Learning SQL Queries for R Users

Request the Database to Furnish Only the Specific Data You Require

Visualize Data Model

Explore and Identify Metadata

Build and Test Query Incrementally

Wrap and Secure Query as Database View

Deploy View in R

Table of Contents

Introduction

The book title implies that *Learning SQL Queries for R Users* is for R users who need to load SQL data into R.

Loading SQL Data into R

The following R snippet shows how we load SQL data, using ROracle package, into R workspace.

The SQL Select statement that retrieves the data is written in **bold** in the R snippet. The statement is imbedded in the R command as a parameter of the dbSendQuery method.

```
> library('ROracle')
> drv <- dbDriver("Oracle")
> con <- dbConnect
(drv,"djoni","pw","host:1521/db")
>
> q <- dbGetQuery(con,"SELECT * FROM product")
>
> class(q)
[1] "data.frame"
>
> q
  P_CODE      P_NAME PRICE   LAUNCH_DT
1      1        Nail    10  2013-03-31
2      2      Washer    15  2013-03-29
3      3         Nut    15  2013-03-29
4      4       Screw    25  2013-03-30
5      5   Super_Nut    30  2013-03-30
6      6     New_Nut    NA        <NA>
>
```

In the above example the SELECT statement retrieves all data from one table only, the product table. (SQL data is stored as one or more tables. A table has columns and rows. In the example, the product table has five columns and six rows.)

ROracle package has a method to retrieve all data from one table, the dbReadTable method. The method simply requires us to supply the name of the table, PRODUCT in our example.

```
> library('ROracle')
> drv <- dbDriver("Oracle")
> con <- dbConnect
(drv,"djoni","pw","host:1521/db")
>
> q <- dbReadTable(con,"PRODUCT")
> q
  P_CODE     P_NAME PRICE  LAUNCH_DT
1      1       Nail    10 2013-03-31
2      2     Washer    15 2013-03-29
3      3        Nut    15 2013-03-29
4      4      Screw    25 2013-03-30
5      5  Super_Nut    30 2013-03-30
6      6    New_Nut    NA       <NA>
>
```

But, a real-world system typically has tens or hundreds of tables. And, the data you need is rarely stored in just one table.

Let's say, we are doing a data mining exercise that requires data not only from a sales table that has the financial figures and sales periods, but also data about product residing on another table, specifically launched date, and yet some other data about customer, specifically address and classification. Additionally, we would like to analyze only the last three years sales data. Assume these required data have to be retrieved from three tables.

If we retrieve the whole data from all three tables, they contain a lot of unnecessary data. Loading high volume data into R can be slow and even prohibitive, due to for example limited R workspace memory.

Instead of loading all data we can write a query to precisely select only the data required. Our query will then look like the following.

```
SELECT price, qty, order_dt, p_name, c_name,
city, prov
FROM product p JOIN c_order co ON p.p_code =
co.p_code
JOIN customer c ON c.c_no = co.c_no
WHERE to_char(order_dt, 'DD-MM-YYYY') >=
to_char(add_months(SYSDATE, -36), 'DD-MM-YYYY')
```

Maintaining a query can be challenging, as the database is unlikely static. A change, as small as the name of a column, if the column is in the SELECT statement, impacts the statement; you must update it inside the R command. A bigger change can be a nightmare, such as when several columns move to different new tables.

Database View

Fortunately, relational database (such as the Oracle database that we use in this book), which maintains the SQL data, has a feature called database view (view for short).

A view wraps a query, which can be as complex as you want. When you use a view the SELECT statement is executed producing our selected data. A view then can be regarded as a custom table and used as the parameter of the dbReadTable method.

A view is a database object created and stored in the database. Once we write and test our query, we then create a view to wrap the query. For example, we create a view named lst_3yrs_sales by executing the following SQL statement.

```
CREATE VIEW lst_3yrs_sales AS
SELECT price, qty, order_dt, p_name, c_name,
city, prov
FROM product p JOIN c_order co ON p.p_code =
co.p_code
JOIN customer c ON c.c_no = co.c_no
WHERE to_char(order_dt, 'DD-MM-YYYY') >=
to_char(add_months(SYSDATE, -36), 'DD-MM-YYYY')
```

R can now use the view as if it is a table as follows.

```
> library('ROracle')
> drv <- dbDriver("Oracle")
> con <- dbConnect(drv, "djoni",
"pw","host:1521/db")
>
> v <- dbReadTable(con,"LST3YRS_SALES")
>
> class(v)
[1] "data.frame"
>
> v
          C_NAME P_NAME PRICE QTY  ORDER_DATE
1  Quality Store   Nail    10 200 01-DEC-2015
2 Standard Store Washer    15 100 01-DEC-2015
3    Head Office    Nut    15 300 15-DEC-2015
4    Super Agent  Screw    25 400 15-DEC-2015
>
```

Identifying the Data

Writing any SELECT statement requires us to identify tables and columns that have the data we need, and the columns to join the tables. We must identify the names of these tables and columns.

Fortunately, we can use GUI facilities of the Oracle SQL Developer, such as the following "Find Database Object".

In the following example, we search all tables and columns that have PR anywhere in their names. The search finds:

- PRODUCT table
- PROV column in the CUSTOMER table
- PRICE column in the PRODUCT table

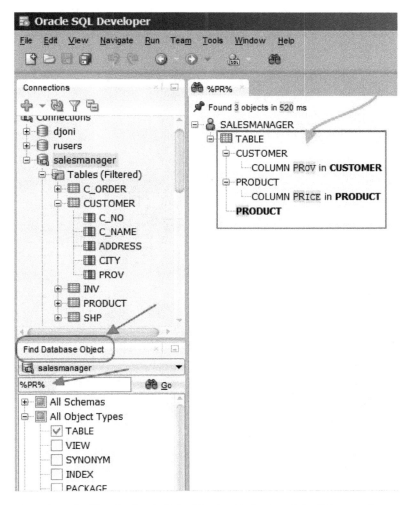

Another facility is the ERD (Entity Relationship Diagram), which can particularly be helpful to visualize the relationships among tables.

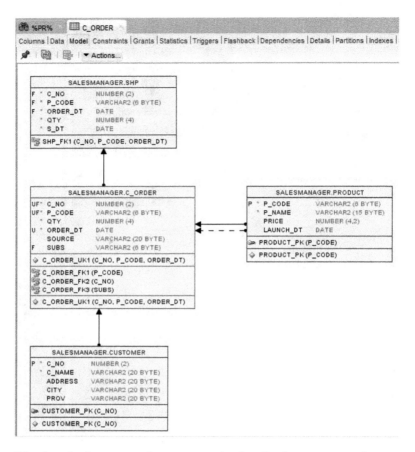

The book shows you how to use in details these two and other GUI facilities.

Purpose of the Book

The book shows you how to identify metadata and data, and build query using the Oracle SQL Developer.

Using examples, the book shows you how to:
- Visualize Data Model
- Explore and Identify Metadata
- Build and Test Query Incrementally
- Wrap and Secure Query as Database View

- Deploy View in R

Even if you will not use view, or your query is not complex that you decide to imbed and maintain SELECT statements directly in R, you still benefit significantly from learning to identify data and build query in the SQL Developer.

You will learn by examples. The example query and its output will be shown in SQL Developer's screen, such as the following. The SELECT statement is on the Worksheet tab and its output on the Query Result tab.

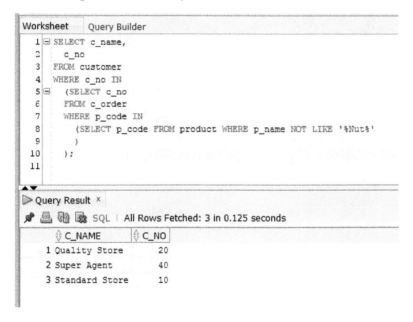

Prerequisite

This book is for R users who want to learn how to write SQL queries. You don't need to have any SQL skill, but you should already be familiar with R as the book does not teach anything about R.

The software's we use in this book are supported in various platforms. We use the Windows installation in this book. You should be familiar with Windows to follow the book examples.

To try the examples, you need to have the followings:
- Oracle SQL Developer and the Database Express Edition. Appendix A guides you to get and install them.
- To try a query and view inside R, you must have set up R and ROracle package.

You must do the preparation before you can try the book examples by following the guide in Appendix B. The guide steps you through creating the database accounts, tables and the data.

SQL Dialects

Though the industry has SQL standard, vendors add unique features to their database, resulting in SQL dialects. SQL statements written for one database may not necessarily work in others.

All SQL query examples in this book are written and tested to correctly run on the Oracle database Express Edition version 11.

Part I: Learning and Writing Queries

All queries regardless of their complexity use the SELECT statement, which has the following basic syntax.

```
SELECT column_names
FROM table_name
WHERE condition;
```

Note that SQL has plenty types of statement, SELECT are just one of them. As this book is about writing queries to retrieve selected data for loading into R, in this book you will use SELECT only. The only other statement that we will use a bit is the CREATE VIEW, which you will learn in the last chapter of this Part I (Chapter 9).

Here is a simple example of a SELECT statement.

```
SELECT price, qty, order_dt, p_name, c_name,
city, prov
FROM product
WHERE p_name <> 'Guava'
to_char(order_dt, 'DD-MM-YYYY') >=
to_char(add_months(SYSDATE, -36), 'DD-MM-YYYY')
```

You see from the above syntax and example that we need the **table name** (product) and **column names**, and **data**, such as the 'Guava' in the example. Additionally, if we have to get the data from more than one table, we also need the **common column names** to join the tables. (You will learn join in Chapter 6)

So, in Part I, we assume we already know the names of the table, table relationships, and if required, the data and the join common columns. **If you in your real-world environment you do not have this information, then you can use the SQL Developer facilities to identify the information. You can learn the facilities in Part II of this book.**

Trying the Book Examples

When you try the examples, you will enter (type) a query (SELECT statement) on the *worksheet* and run the query by clicking the green arrow head *Run Statement* button.

Note that we will not use a facility in the SQL Developer named Query Builder, which can only be effective for building very simple queries.

As an example of what you will see for all the book examples, here is a SQL Developer screenshot showing the query and its output.

- The **SELECT * FROM product** statement is typed in on the *djoni* worksheet.
- The query output is displayed on the Query Result panel.

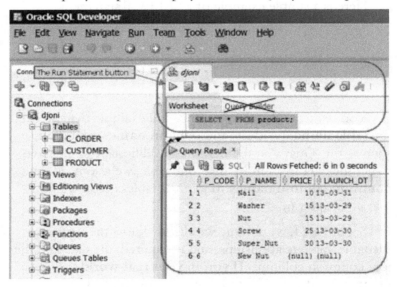

The *salesmanager* Schema

The following ERD shows the five tables in the *salesmanager* schema we will use in the examples.

If you need to know how to read (interpret) this ERD, please consult "Reading ERD" in Chapter 11.

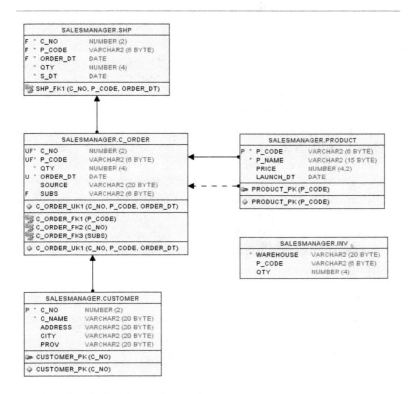

Notice the followings about the ERD.

- The C_ORDER table relates to the PRODUCT table **twice**.
  - One of the relations, the mandatory one (the solid arrow), has P_CODE on both tables as common columns of the relationship.
  - The other, which is not mandatory (the dotted arrow), has the C_ORDER's SUBS column and PRODUCT's P_CODE column as the relationship's common columns. The SUBS column is for a substitute product to the product of this order. You

use common columns to join the two tables. You will learn joins in Chapter 6.

- The INV table should have been related to the C_ORDER table with common columns WAREHOUSE and SOURCE respectively. Instead we make it a standalone table, it does not relate to any other table, in the book example for our learning. Sometimes, in a real-world environment, you encounter this kind of standalone table, which makes you difficult to find out to correctly join the table to other tables that should have been related.
- The C_ORDER table does not have any primary key. Instead it has a unique key that is composed of three columns: P_CODE, C_NO, and ORDER_DT. These three columns form the common column part of the table that we use to join to the SHP table (SHP is an abbreviation of SHIPPING). We will use the SHP table in the **No Foreign/Primary Key Relationship** section of Chapter 6.

The Tables

The followings show the rows of our example tables.

	P_CODE	P_NAME	PRICE	LAUNCH_DT
1	1	Nail	10	15-03-31
2	2	Washer	15	13-03-29
3	3	Nut	15	13-03-29
4	4	Screw	25	13-03-30
5	5	Super_Nut	30	13-03-30
6	6	New Nut	(null)	(null)

PRODUCT

Columns Data Model Constraints Grants Statistics T

Sort.. Filter:

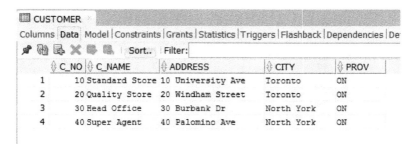

CUSTOMER

Columns | Data | Model | Constraints | Grants | Statistics | Triggers | Flashback | Dependencies | De

Sort.. | Filter:

	C_NO	C_NAME	ADDRESS	CITY	PROV
1	10	Standard Store	10 University Ave	Toronto	ON
2	20	Quality Store	20 Windham Street	Toronto	ON
3	30	Head Office	30 Burbank Dr	North York	ON
4	40	Super Agent	40 Palomino Ave	North York	ON

INV

Columns | Data | Model | Constraints | Grants | S

Sort.. | Filter:

	WAREHOUSE	P_CODE	QTY
1	1	1	100
2	2	2	200

C_ORDER

Columns | Data | Model | Constraints | Grants | Statistics | Trigger

Sort.. | Filter:

	C_NO	P_CODE	QTY	ORDER_DT	SOURCE
1	10	1	100	13-04-01	1
2	10	2	100	13-04-01	1
3	20	1	200	13-04-01	2
4	30	3	300	13-04-02	2
5	40	4	400	13-04-02	(null)
6	40	5	400	13-04-03	(null)

SHP

Columns | Data | Model | Constraints | Grants | Statistics | Triggers |

Sort.. | Filter:

	C_NO	P_CODE	ORDER_DT	QTY	S_DT
1	10	1	13-04-01	100	13-04-05
2	10	2	13-04-01	100	13-04-05

[14]

Chapter 1: Tables and Columns

Let's begin by reviewing how data is organized in SQL database.

Data in SQL database, such as the Oracle database (the one we use in this book) is stored as tables. A simple sales database, for example, might have five tables that contain data about product, customer, customer order, inventory, and warehouse.

- A record of data is a row of the table.
  - o To query the rows you must know the name of the table.
- A row has columns.
  - o To select the columns you want to include in the output of a query you must know the name of the columns.
- Every table should have a column (or multiple columns together) designated as the primary key or unique key of the table. A column of another table can be designated as a foreign key that references the primary or unique key.
  - o The primary key/foreign key columns relate the two tables.
  - o In a query, you use these columns to join rows from the two tables.

Data Types

You need to know the data types of the columns to correctly manipulate the data in R.

The following screenshot show the data types of the columns of our product table. (This is a screenshot from SQL Developer. You will learn how to display tables and columns, and other information about data, in the next chapters)

```
 PRODUCT
Columns Data | Model | Constraints | Grants | Stat
       ▼ Actions...
      COLUMN_NAME    DATA_TYPE
  1 P_CODE          VARCHAR2(6 BYTE)
  2 P_NAME          VARCHAR2(15 BYTE)
  3 PRICE           NUMBER(4,2)
  4 LAUNCH_DT       DATE
```

In addition to the data types used above, Oracle supports other data types.

Here is a list of the Oracle data types.

Data Type	Description
VARCHAR2(*ml*)	Variable-length character string having a maximum length of *ml*
NVARCHAR2(*ml*)	The Unicode version of VARCHAR2
NUMBER(*p, s*)	Number having precision *p* and scale *s*
DATE	Valid date ranging from January 1, 4712 BC, to December 31, 9999 AD
BINARY_FLOAT	32-bit floating point number
BINARY_DOUBLE	64-bit floating point number
TIMESTAMP	The year, month, and day values of the date, plus the hour, minute, and second values of the time
INTERVAL YEAR	Stores a period of time in years and months
INTERVAL DAY	Stores a period of time in days, hours, minutes, and seconds
RAW(*size*)	Raw binary data of the length of *size* bytes
LONG RAW	The larger version of RAW
ROWID	Base-64 string representing the unique address of a row in its table
CHAR(*l*)	Fixed-length character string having length *l*
NCHAR(*l*)	Unicode version of CHAR
CLOB	A character large object containing single-bytes or multi-byte characters
NCLOB	Unicode version of CLOB
BLOB	A binary large object
BFILE	Contains the locator to a large binary file stored outside the database

Having access to the database and understanding how data is stored in the database, we will next use SQL Developer to identify tables, columns, and table relationships.

Chapter 2: Query Basics

If you have not done so, start your SQL Developer and connect to the database using the *ruser* account. (Consult Appendix B about this account)

Let us now begin your journey to learn SQL queries.

Here is again the SELECT statement.

```
SELECT column_names FROM table_name [WHERE
condition];
```

Only the SELECT and FROM clauses are mandatory. If your query does not have a WHERE clause, the result will include all rows in the table. If your query has a WHERE clause then only the rows satisfying the WHERE condition will be returned.

The simplest query, which reads all data (all rows and all columns) from a table, has the following syntax.

```
SELECT * FROM table;
```

The asterisk (*) means all columns in the table. For instance, the following query retrieves all data from the product table.

If your table has lots of rows, the query will take a long time to finish before it begins to show its output rows.

Worksheet	Query Builder
1	select * from product;

▲▼

▷ Query Result ×

📌 🖨 🔁 📇 SQL | All Rows Fetched: 6 in 0 seconds

	P_CODE	P_NAME	PRICE	LAUNCH_DT
1	1	Nail	10	31-MAR-15
2	2	Washer	15	29-MAR-13
3	3	Nut	15	29-MAR-13
4	4	Screw	25	30-MAR-13
5	5	Super_Nut	30	30-MAR-13
6	6	New Nut	(null)	(null)

SQL statement is not case sensitive. The *SELECT * from product* is the same as *select * FROM product*, and also the same as *SELECT * from PRODUCT*.

If the table has more rows you need to scroll down the query result.
- Use the Page-Up and –Down keys of your keyboard, Home and End.
- If your table has lots of rows, pressing End might take a while to see the last rows.

Note that some of the types of queries you learn in this chapter will seldom be your final queries that you use to load data into R. You will use these queries mostly to explore data, kind of the preliminaries before start writing the actual query.

You might never implement the preceding query, for example, as it retrieves the whole table. You learn this type of query and some that follow to build your SQL query writing incrementally, which you can do comfortably in SQL Developer.

Selected Columns

To query specific columns, list the columns in the SELECT clause.

- You write the columns in the order you want to see them in the output table.
- You can list all columns arranged in the order you want.

Here's an example (the second SELECT statement):

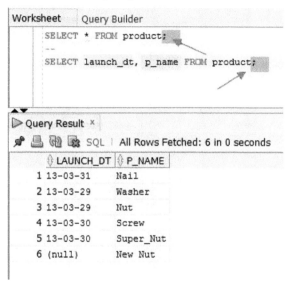

Notice that you can have more than one statement in the worksheet.

- Make sure every statement ends with a semicolon ;
- The double dashes in between the two statements, which is optional, is a comment line, not executable, used here to visually delineate the statements.
- Place your cursor on the statement you want to execute.
- The "Query Result" panel shows only the output rows of the executed statement.

You can clear up the worksheet by clicking the Clear button; all statements will be deleted, no longer available even from the clipboard.

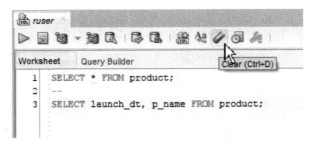

You can recall successfully executed SQL statement from the history. If you click F8 the SQL History panel will be shown.

Double-click the statement that you want to recall and it will be pasted on the worksheet that you can edit and/or execute.

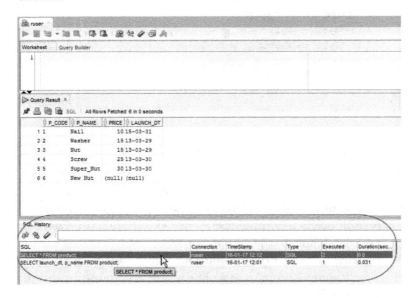

You can have multiple Query Result panels.

- Having multiple output panels one for each query can be helpful to compare different versions of a query during its incremental development.
- Query Result panel has a name (label). Default name is "Query Result"
- You should rename an existing panel from Query Result to a unique name among the panels before executing another query.

To rename a panel, right click on the panel, and then select Rename.

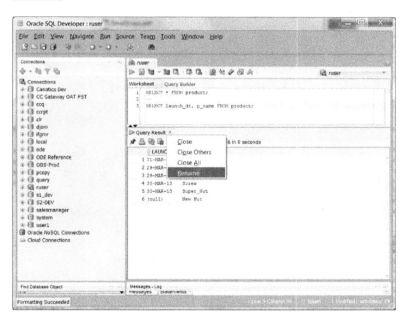

Enter a new name to replace the default Query Result, and then click the Apply button.
- The new name must be unique among the tabs.
- The new name should briefly describe the query, e.g. its output or purpose.

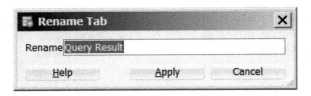

A new Query Result panel (tab) will have the output rows of the next query just executed.

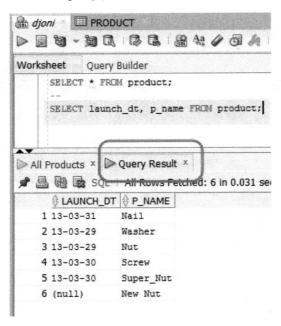

Saving query result

You might want to save the output rows.

- Right-click on any of the output rows, and then select Export.

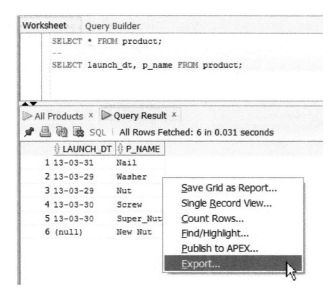

On the next window:
- You can choose one of the available output formats, e.g. csv (comma separated values) or xls (Excel)
- Designate the file and its folder where you want to store the export, and then click the Next button.

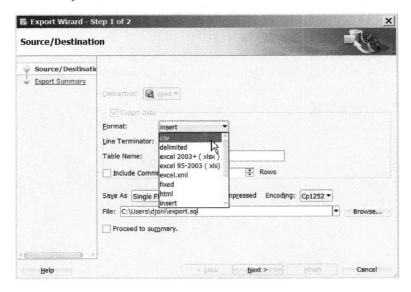

Then on the next window, click the Finish button. The export file should be available on the designated folder.

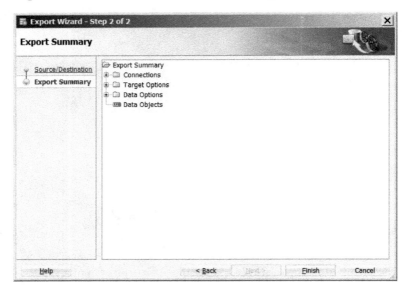

Limiting the Number of Returned Rows

If the table has a lot of rows while you only want to have a feel about the data by seeing only some first few rows, you can issue the following SQL.

- ROWNUM is a pseudo column (not a column from the queried table), contains a sequential integer assigned by the Oracle database to the rows returned by a query.
- You will see the first n-1 returned rows by the query.

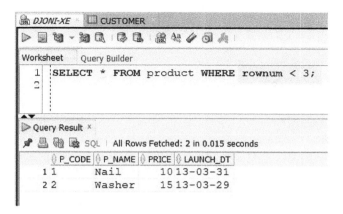

A variation of the above is to retrieve a range of rows based on the ROWNUM.

The following query gives you row number 2, 3 and 4.
- This is a query that has a subquery.
  - A subquery, also called inner query, is a query under another query.
  - You will learn subquery in a later chapter.
  - Remember this: The output of a query (any query, including subquery) is a transient table, it is not stored in the database likes the 'normal' table.
- The inner query selects all rows and all columns of the product table.
  - The output column includes ROWNUM aliased rn.
  - You will learn more about column alias in later chapter.
- The outer query then using the rn column of the subquery's output rows produces row number 2, 3, and 4.
  - You will learn BETWEEN in later chapter.

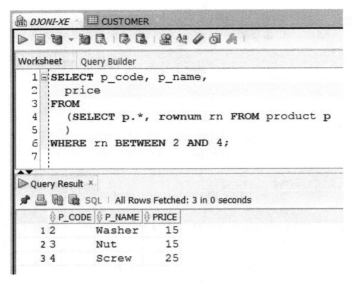

The following query selects the top two products as a result of their highest price.

- The inner query orders the rows by price descending and NULL is placed last.
- The outer query then picks the top two of the inner query output rows.

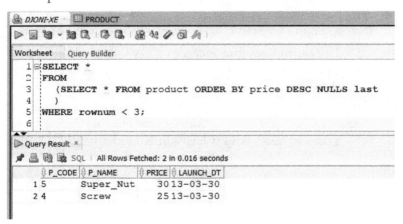

DISTINCT

Use the DISTINCT to find out the available values in a
column or across multiple columns.

■ A value will be listed once only.

Single Column

The following query will result in a list of prices.

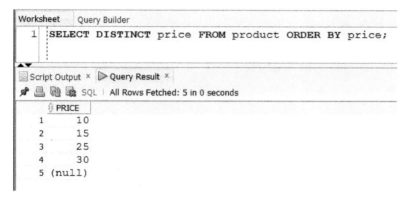

Multiple Columns

If a query returns multiple columns, two rows are considered
duplicates if all their columns have the same values.

■ They are not duplicates if only one column has the same
   value.
■ For example, the following query applies DISTINCT on
   two columns.

```
Worksheet    Query Builder
   1  SELECT DISTINCT price, launch_dt FROM product ORDER BY price;
```

```
Script Output ×  ▷ Query Result ×
   SQL | All Rows Fetched: 5 in 0.031 seconds
     PRICE   LAUNCH_DT
   1      10 13-03-31
   2      15 13-03-29
   3      25 13-03-30
   4      30 13-03-30
   5 (null) (null)
```

LIKE

Using LIKE you can specify an imprecise equality condition. The syntax is as follows.

```
SELECT columns FROM table
WHERE column LIKE ' ... wildcard_character ...
';
```

The wildcard character can be a percentage sign (%) to represent any number of characters or an underscore (_) to represent a single occurrence of any character.

The next query uses the LIKE operator on the p_name.

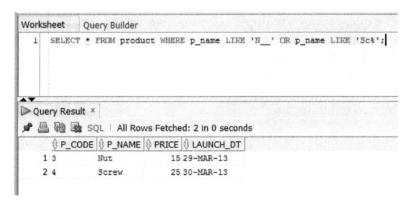

```
Worksheet    Query Builder
   1  SELECT * FROM product WHERE p_name LIKE 'N__' OR p_name LIKE 'Sc%';
```

```
▷ Query Result ×
   SQL | All Rows Fetched: 2 in 0 seconds
     P_CODE  P_NAME  PRICE  LAUNCH_DT
   1 3       Nut        15 29-MAR-13
   2 4       Screw      25 30-MAR-13
```

Even though you can use LIKE for numeric columns, it is primarily used with columns of type string.

ESCAPE

If the string you specify in the LIKE operator contains underscore or percentage sign, SQL will regard it as a wild character.

For example, if you want to query products that have an underscore in their names, your SQL statement would look like the following.

```
SELECT * FROM product WHERE p_name LIKE '%_%';
```

But, the query will return all rows instead of just the Super_Nut, because the underscore in the LIKE operator is regarded as a wild card character, i.e. any one character.

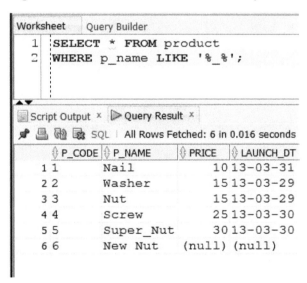

Use ESCAPE to resolve the issue, as in the following example. In the statement the ESCAPE clause defines \ (backslash) as an escape character, meaning any character in the LIKE operator after a backslash will be considered a character, not as a wildcard character.

Now only rows whose p_name contains an underscore will be returned.

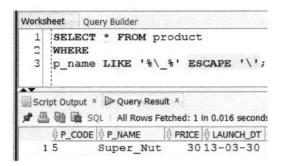

Chapter 3: Selecting Rows

You use the WHERE clause to select specific rows.

The following SQL statement queries the p_name and price from the product table with price = 15.

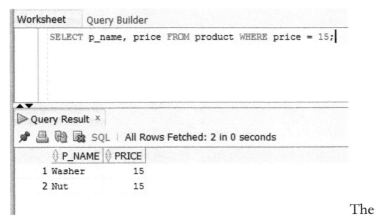

The equal sign (=) in the WHERE condition is one of the comparison operators. Here's a list of all comparison operators.

Operator	Description
=	Equal to
<	Less than
>	Greater than
<=	Less than or equal to
>=	Greater than or equal to
!=	Not equal to

Here is another example using the not equal to (!=) operator to select rows where the product name is not equal to Nut.

```
Worksheet    Query Builder
     SELECT p_name, price FROM product WHERE p_name != 'Nut';
```

Query Result ×

SQL | All Rows Fetched: 5 in 0.016 seconds

	P_NAME	PRICE
1	Nail	10
2	Washer	15
3	Screw	25
4	Super_Nut	30
5	New Nut	(null)

Compound Conditions

The condition p_name != 'Nut' is called a predicate. Using the AND and OR logical operator you can combine predicates to form a compound condition.

The rules for the OR logical operator are as follows.

Left condition	Logical operator	Right condition	Compound condition
True	OR	True	True
True	OR	False	True
False	OR	True	True
False	OR	False	False

In principle, the result of the OR compound condition is true (satisfying the condition) if any one of the two conditions being OR-ed is true; otherwise, if none of the conditions is true, the compound condition is false (not satisfying the condition).

The rules for the AND logical operator are presented in Table 2.3.

Left condition	Logical operator	Right condition	Compound condition

True	AND	True	True
True	AND	False	FALSE
False	AND	True	FALSE
False	AND	False	FALSE

Basically, the result of the AND compound condition is true only if the two conditions being AND-ed are true; otherwise, the result is false.

The following SQL statement contains three predicates compounded.

The result of the first compound condition (TO_CHAR(launch_dt, 'DD-MON-YY') >= '30-MAR-13' OR price > 15) is true for Nail, Screw and Super_Nut rows in the product table; AND-ing this result with the (p_name != 'Nail') predicate results in two products, the Screw and Super_Nut.

Note the use of TO_CHAR to convert the launch_dt into a character string with the DD-MM-YY format. TO_CHAR is one of the many built-in functions provided by the Oracle database. Appendix D has some other of the other built-in functions. To see the all built-in functions, please consult the product documentation available on the Oracle website.

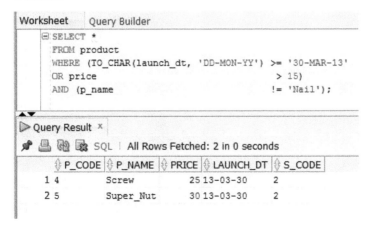

Note that New Nut does not satisfy the condition because applying any of the comparison operators to NULL results in false (the price and launch_dt of the New Nut are NULL). The section "Handling NULL" later in this chapter explains more about NULL.

Evaluation Precedence and the Use of Parentheses

If a compound condition contains both the OR condition and the AND condition, the AND condition will be evaluated first because AND has a higher precedence than OR. However, anything in parentheses will have an even higher precedence than AND.

In the previous query the SELECT statement has an OR and an AND, but the OR condition is in parentheses so the OR condition is evaluated first. If you remove the parentheses (as in the next SQL statement) the query will return a different result.

Without the parentheses, the compound condition price > 15 AND p_name != 'Nail' will be evaluated first, resulting in the Screw and Super_Nut. The result is then OR-ed with the launch_dt >= 30-MAR-13' condition, resulting in these three rows.

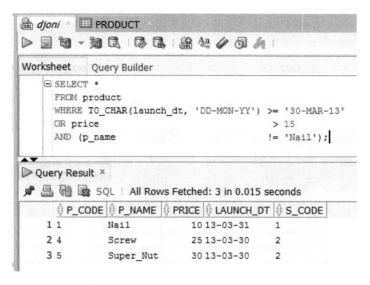

The NOT Logical Operator

You can use NOT to negate a condition and return rows that do not satisfy the condition as in the following query.

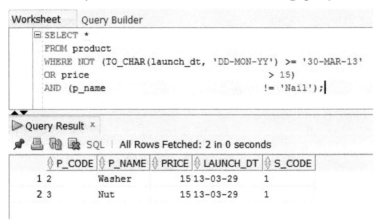

While in the previous query the NOT is applied to the whole condition, the following query has a NOT applied only to the last predicate.

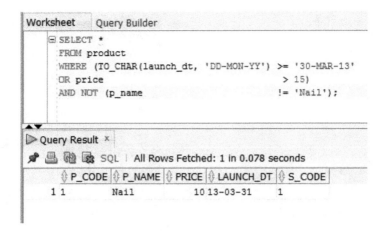

The BETWEEN Operator

The BETWEEN operator evaluates equality to any value within a range. The range is specified by a boundary, which specifies the lowest and the highest values.

Here is the syntax for BETWEEN.

```
SELECT columns FROM table
WHERE column BETWEEN(lowest_value,
highest_value);
```

The boundary values are inclusive, meaning *lowest_value* and *highest_value* will be included in the equality evaluation.

Here is an example.

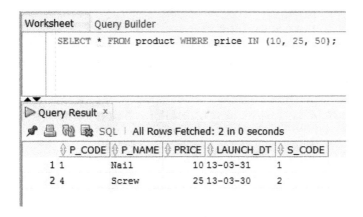

The IN Operator

The IN operator compares a column with a list of values. The syntax for a query that uses IN is as follows.

```
SELECT columns FROM table
WHERE column IN(value1, value2, ...);
```

The following query uses IN.

Combining the NOT operator

You can combine NOT with BETWEEN, IN, or LIKE to negate their conditions.

The following query combines NOT with BETWEEN.

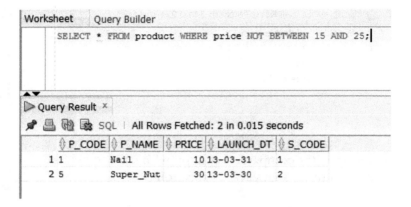

Handling NULL

NULL, an SQL reserved word, represents the absence of data.

- NULL is applicable to any data type.
- It is not a numeric zero or an empty string or a 0000/00/00 date.
- The result of applying any of the comparison operators on NULL is always NULL; hence use the IS NULL or IS NOT NULL operator.
- **NA in R is the equivalent of NULL. When loaded into R, NULL is translated to NA.**

As an example, the following query will produce no output.

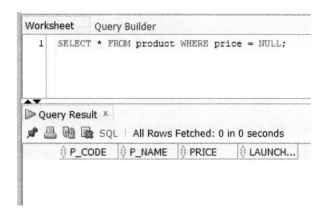

The following query uses the IS NULL operator

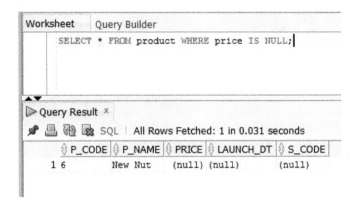

Chapter 4: Query Output

Your query does not need to return column as-is from the tables. You can for example rename column and produce calculated column.

Column Aliases

By default the names of the query output are the names of the columns from the table. You can give them aliases.

The syntax for the SELECT clause that uses aliases is as follows.

```
SELECT column_1 AS alias1,
column_2 AS alias2, ...
FROM table;
```

- The AS is optional.
- An alias can consist of one or multiple words.
- You must enclose a multiword alias with quotes, e.g. "Product Name".
- The quotes preserve the upper/lower-case of the word(s)

Here's an example.

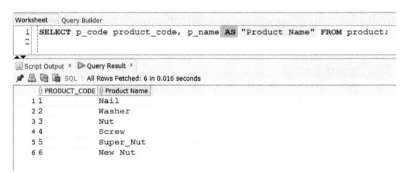

Expressions

An output column can also be an expression. An expression in the SELECT clause can include columns, literal values, arithmetic or string operators, and functions.

The following is an example.

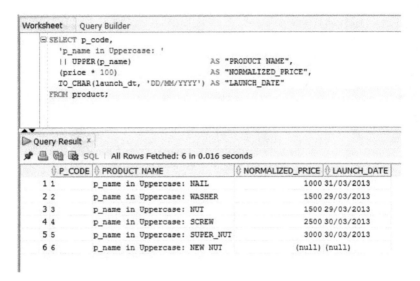

You can use other arithmetic operators in addition to the multiplication (*) operator in your column. These include addition (+), subtraction (-), and division (/)

Aggregate Functions

You can manipulate your query output further by using aggregate functions. The aggregate functions are listed below.

Function	Description
MAX(column)	The maximum column value
MIN(column)	The minimum column value
SUM(column)	The sum of column values
AVG(column)	The average column value
COUNT(column)	The count of rows

COUNT(*)	The count of all rows including NULL.

As an example, the following query uses the six aggregate functions.

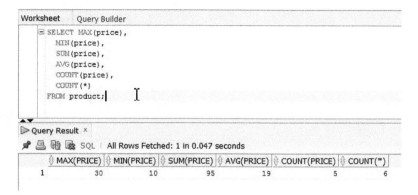

CASE

Use CASE to build logic in the SELECT statement.

- CASE comes in two flavours: simple and searched.

The Simple CASE

The syntax for the simple CASE is as follows.

```
SELECT columns,
  CASE column
    WHEN equal_value1
    THEN output_value1
    WHEN equal_value2
    THEN output_value2
    WHEN ...
    [ELSE else_value]
  END AS output_column
FROM table
WHERE ... ;
```

column_name is compared to equal_values, starting from the first WHEN and down to the last WHEN.

Only one of the output_value's or NULL is returned according to the following logic.

- If *column_name* matches a WHEN value, the value right after the THEN clause is returned and the CASE process stops.
- If *column_name* matches none of the WHEN values, *else_value* is returned.
- If *column_name* matches none of the WHEN values but no ELSE clause exists, NULL will be returned.

The following query uses a simple CASE for the price column to produce a price_cat (price category) output column.

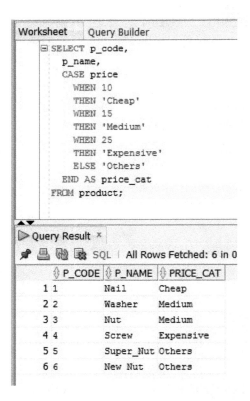

The Searched CASE

While the simple CASE compares a column with various values, the searched CASE can be any condition. The syntax for the searched CASE is as follows.

```
SELECT columns,
  CASE
    WHEN condition1
    THEN output_value1
    WHEN condition2
    THEN output_value2
    WHEN ...
    ELSE else_value
  END AS output_column
FROM table
WHERE ... ;
```

The conditions are evaluated starting from the first WHEN and down to the last
- If a WHEN condition is met, its THEN output_value is returned to the output_column and the CASE process stops.
- If none of the WHEN conditions is met, *else_value* is returned if there exists an ELSE clause.
- If no condition is met and no ELSE clause exists, NULL will be returned.

The following query uses a searched CASE.
- While the previous simple CASE categorized the products based on only their prices, this searched CASE categorizes the products based on the various conditions which can involve more than just the price.
- In the searched CASE, NULL equality can be a condition, something that is not allowed in the Simple CASE.

```
Worksheet    Query Builder
  1 ⊟ SELECT p_code,
  2      p_name,
  3      CASE
  4        WHEN (price <= 10
  5        AND p_name NOT LIKE 'Nut%')
  6        THEN 'Cheap'
  7        WHEN price BETWEEN 11 AND 25
  8        THEN 'Medium'
  9        WHEN price > 25 and TO_CHAR(launch_dt, 'YYYYMMDD') > '20130329'
 10        THEN 'Expensive'
 11        WHEN price IS NULL
 12        THEN 'Not valid'
 13        ELSE 'Others'
 14      END AS product_cat
 15   FROM product;
 16
```

▷ Query Result ×

📌 🖨 🔢 📑 SQL | All Rows Fetched: 6 in 0 seconds

	P_CODE	P_NAME	PRODUCT_CAT
1	1	Nail	Cheap
2	2	Washer	Medium
3	3	Nut	Medium
4	4	Screw	Medium
5	5	Super_Nut	Expensive
6	6	New Nut	Not valid

Ordering Output Rows

You can order the output rows using the ORDER BY clause.
- The ORDER BY clause must appear last in a SELECT statement.

Here is the syntax for a query having the ORDER BY clause.

```
SELECT columns FROM
table
WHERE condition ORDER BY column(s)
```

We will show examples of the following varieties of ordering.

- by one or more columns
- in ascending or descending direction
- by using the GROUP BY clause
- by using UNION and other set operators

Ordering by One Column

The simplest is ordering by one column.

Worksheet	Query Builder

```
SELECT * FROM product ORDER BY p_name;
```

Query Result ×

SQL All Rows Fetched: 6 in 0.032 seconds

	P_CODE	P_NAME	PRICE	LAUNCH_DT	S_CODE
1	1	Nail	10	13-03-31	1
2	6	New Nut	(null)	(null)	(null)
3	3	Nut	15	13-03-29	1
4	4	Screw	25	13-03-30	2
5	5	Super_Nut	30	13-03-30	2
6	2	Washer	15	13-03-29	1

Direction of Order

The default direction is ascending. To order a column in descending direction, use the DESC reserved word.

In the following query, the output rows will be returned with p_name sorted in descending order.

Worksheet	Query Builder
	SELECT * FROM product ORDER BY p_name DESC; I

▶ Query Result ×

📌 🖨 🔖 📋 SQL | All Rows Fetched: 6 in 0.031 seconds

	P_CODE	P_NAME	PRICE	LAUNCH_DT	S_CODE
1	2	Washer	15	13-03-29	1
2	5	Super_Nut	30	13-03-30	2
3	4	Screw	25	13-03-30	2
4	3	Nut	15	13-03-29	1
5	6	New Nut	(null)	(null)	(null)
6	1	Nail	10	13-03-31	1

Multiple Columns

To order by more than one column, list the columns in the ORDER BY clause.

The sequence of columns listed is significant.
- The order will be by the first column in the list, followed by the second column, and so on.
- For example, if the ORDER BY clause has two columns, the query output will first be ordered by the first column. Any rows with identical values in the first column will be further ordered by the second column.

In the following query, the output rows will first be ordered by launch_dt and then by price, both in ascending order. The secondary ordering by price is seen on the Screw and Super_Nut rows. Their launch_dt's are the same, 30-MAR-13. Their prices are different, Screw's lower than Super_Nut's, hence Screw row comes before the Super_Nut.

Worksheet	Query Builder

```
SELECT * FROM product ORDER BY launch_dt, price;
```

▶ Query Result ×

📌 🖨 🕷 🖼 SQL All Rows Fetched: 6 in 0.031 seconds

	P_CODE	P_NAME	PRICE	LAUNCH_DT	S_CODE
1	3	Nut	15	13-03-29	1
2	2	Washer	15	13-03-29	1
3	4	Screw	25	13-03-30	2
4	5	Super_Nut	30	13-03-30	2
5	1	Nail	10	13-03-31	1
6	6	New Nut	(null)	(null)	(null)

Different Directions on Different Columns

You can apply different order directions on different columns.

In the following query, the output rows will be ordered by launch_dt in ascending order and then by price in descending order. Now, the Super_Nut comes before the Screw.

Worksheet	Query Builder
	SELECT * FROM product ORDER BY launch_dt ASC, price DESC;

▲▼

▷ Query Result ×

📌 🖨 🐍 🐍 SQL | All Rows Fetched: 6 in 0.016 seconds

	P_CODE	P_NAME	PRICE	LAUNCH_DT	S_CODE
1	3	Nut	15	13-03-29	1
2	2	Washer	15	13-03-29	1
3	5	Super_Nut	30	13-03-30	2
4	4	Screw	25	13-03-30	2
5	1	Nail	10	13-03-31	1
6	6	New Nut	(null)	(null)	(null)

Ordering with a WHERE clause

If your SELECT statement has both the WHERE clause and the ORDER BY clause, ORDER BY must appear after the WHERE clause.

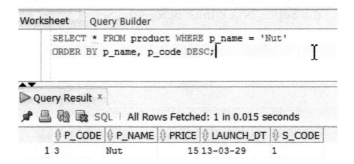

Worksheet	Query Builder
	SELECT * FROM product WHERE p_name = 'Nut' ORDER BY p_name, p_code DESC;

▲▼

▷ Query Result ×

📌 🖨 🐍 🐍 SQL | All Rows Fetched: 1 in 0.015 seconds

	P_CODE	P_NAME	PRICE	LAUNCH_DT	S_CODE
1	3	Nut	15	13-03-29	1

Chapter 5: Grouping

A group is a set of rows having the same value on specific columns.

In the previous chapter you learned how to apply aggregate functions on all output rows. In this chapter you learn how to create groups and apply aggregate functions on those groups.

The GROUP BY Clause

In a query the GROUP BY clause appears after the WHERE clause and before the ORDER clause, if any. Here is the syntax for a SELECT statement with the WHERE, GROUP BY, and ORDER BY clauses.

```
SELECT columns,
    aggregate_function(group_columns)
FROM table(s)
WHERE condition
GROUP BY group_columns
ORDER BY column(s);
```

The following query groups the output from the product table by their launch date.

The query output will have four rows, one for each of the four grouped launch dates.
- The COUNT(price) element, which counts the rows with a value on their price column, produces 0.
- On the other hand, the COUNT(*) element, which counts the NULL launch dates, produces 1.

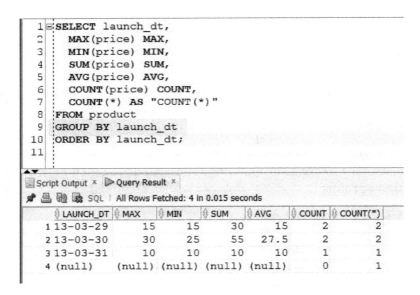

You can group by more than one column.

- If you do that, rows having the same value on all the columns will form a group.
- The following query group the rows by price and launch date.

Though the Screw and Super_Nut have the same price, they have different launch dates, and therefore they form different groups.

```
Worksheet   Query Builder
1  ⊟SELECT price, launch_dt,
2      MAX(price) MAX, MIN(price) MIN,
3      SUM(price) SUM, AVG(price) AVG,
4      COUNT(price) COUNT, COUNT(*) "COUNT(*)"
5  FROM product
6  GROUP BY price, launch_dt
7  ORDER BY price, launch_dt;
8
```

Script Output × ▷ Query Result ×

📌 🖨 🔊 📑 SQL | All Rows Fetched: 5 in 0 seconds

	PRICE	LAUNCH_DT	MAX	MIN	SUM	AVG	COUNT	COUNT(*)
1	10	13-03-31	10	10	10	10	1	1
2	15	13-03-29	15	15	30	15	2	2
3	25	13-03-30	25	25	25	25	1	1
4	30	13-03-30	30	30	30	30	1	1
5	(null)	(null)	(null)	(null)	(null)	(null)	0	1

The HAVING Keyword

You use the WHERE condition to select individual rows.

On the other hand, the HAVING condition is used for selecting individual groups.

- Only groups that satisfy the condition in the HAVING clause will be returned by the query. In other words, the HAVING condition is on the aggregate, not on a column.
- If present, the HAVING clause must appear after the GROUP BY, as in the following syntax.

```
SELECT columns,
  aggregate_function(group_columns)
FROM table(s)
WHERE condition
GROUP BY group_columns
HAVING aggregate_condition
ORDER BY columns;
```

Here is an example of the HAVING condition.

Only groups having more than one row (satisfying the COUNT(price) > 1 condition) will be returned. Only one row will be returned, the one with price = 15 and launch date = 29-MAR-13.

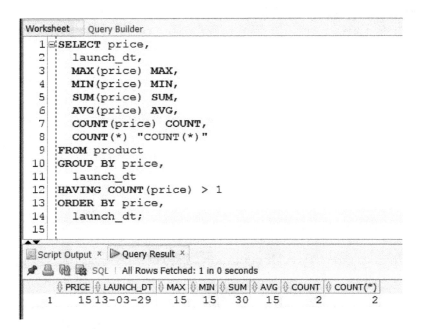

If a WHERE clause is present, it must appear after the GROUP BY clause.

- Individual rows will be selected by the WHERE condition first before grouping occurs.
- For instance, the following query uses both WHERE and GROUP BY.

```
Worksheet    Query Builder
 1  SELECT launch_dt, MAX(price) MAX,
 2     MIN(price) MIN, SUM(price) SUM,
 3     AVG(price) AVG, COUNT(price) COUNT,
 4     COUNT(*) "COUNT(*)"
 5  FROM product
 6  WHERE p_name NOT LIKE 'Super%'
 7  GROUP BY launch_dt
 8  HAVING TO_CHAR(launch_dt, 'DD-MON-YY') > '29-MAR-13'
 9  ORDER BY launch_dt;
10
```

Script Output × ▷ Query Result ×

📌 🖨 🔢 📇 SQL | All Rows Fetched: 2 in 0.016 seconds

	LAUNCH_DT	MAX	MIN	SUM	AVG	COUNT	COUNT(*)
1	13-03-30	25	25	25	25	1	1
2	13-03-31	10	10	10	10	1	1

Chapter 6: Joins

A real-world database typically stores data in dozens or even hundreds of tables where table relates to one or more tables forming network of tables.

In this chapter you will learn how to relate two or more tables to get their related rows.

Here is the ERD of our example tables that you will need to refer to.

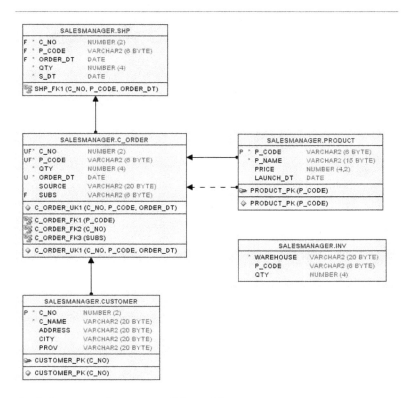

And, here are the rows of the tables.

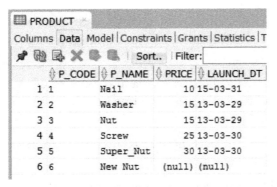

PRODUCT

Columns | Data | Model | Constraints | Grants | Statistics | T

	P_CODE	P_NAME	PRICE	LAUNCH_DT
1	1	Nail	10	15-03-31
2	2	Washer	15	13-03-29
3	3	Nut	15	13-03-29
4	4	Screw	25	13-03-30
5	5	Super_Nut	30	13-03-30
6	6	New Nut	(null)	(null)

CUSTOMER

Columns | Data | Model | Constraints | Grants | Statistics | Triggers | Flashback | Dependencies | De

	C_NO	C_NAME	ADDRESS	CITY	PROV
1	10	Standard Store	10 University Ave	Toronto	ON
2	20	Quality Store	20 Windham Street	Toronto	ON
3	30	Head Office	30 Burbank Dr	North York	ON
4	40	Super Agent	40 Palomino Ave	North York	ON

INV

Columns | Data | Model | Constraints | Grants | S

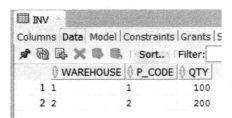

	WAREHOUSE	P_CODE	QTY
1	1	1	100
2	2	2	200

C_ORDER

Columns | Data | Model | Constraints | Grants | Statistics | Trigger

	C_NO	P_CODE	QTY	ORDER_DT	SOURCE
1	10	1	100	13-04-01	1
2	10	2	100	13-04-01	1
3	20	1	200	13-04-01	2
4	30	3	300	13-04-02	2
5	40	4	400	13-04-02	(null)
6	40	5	400	13-04-03	(null)

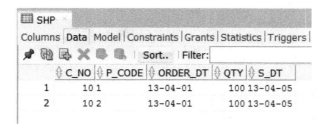

JOIN

To get related rows from two tables, you use JOIN clause in the SELECT statement.

The JOIN syntax is as follows.

```
SELECT table1.column(s), table2.column(s)
FROM table1 JOIN table2
ON table1.column1 = table2.column2
```

- On the ON clause you specify the common columns that relate the tables.
- You can select any output columns from any column of the two tables.
- If columns on different tables have identical names, you must qualify such column with its table. You use dot notation to qualify a column; the . between table and column.

Here is an example query joining C_ORDER and CUSTOMER tables on their c_no columns.

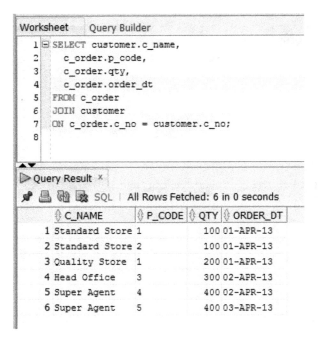

Using Table Aliases

In the following query, o is an alias for the c_order table and c is an alias for the customer table. These aliases are then used in the ON clause to qualify the c_no columns with their respective tables.

- We do not need to qualify the selected columns as they exist in one table only.

```
Worksheet    Query Builder
  1 ⊟ SELECT c_name,
  2       p_code,
  3       o.qty,
  4       o.order_dt
  5    FROM c_order o
  6    JOIN customer c
  7    ON o.c_no = c.c_no;
  8
```

▲▼

▷ Query Result ×

📌 🖨 🔲 📋 SQL All Rows Fetched: 6 in 0.008 seconds

C_NAME	P_CODE	QTY	ORDER_DT
1 Standard Store	1	100	01-APR-13
2 Standard Store	2	100	01-APR-13
3 Quality Store	1	200	01-APR-13
4 Head Office	3	300	02-APR-13
5 Super Agent	4	400	02-APR-13
6 Super Agent	5	400	03-APR-13

Column Aliases vs. Table Aliases

In Chapter 4, "Query Output", you learned that column alias uses AS keyword. Although a column alias can be created without using the AS keyword, its presence improves readability ("p_name AS product_name" instead of "p_name product_name"). On the other hand, table aliases cannot use the AS keyword.

Joining More than Two Tables

From the JOIN syntax presented earlier, you can join more than two tables. To do this, in the SELECT statement, join two tables at a time.

The following example query joins the c_order table to the customer table, and then joins the customer table to the product table. The rows in the c_order table are joined to the rows of the same c_no column from the customer table, and these rows are then joined to the rows with the same p_code from the product table. This query returns the customer names and their orders.

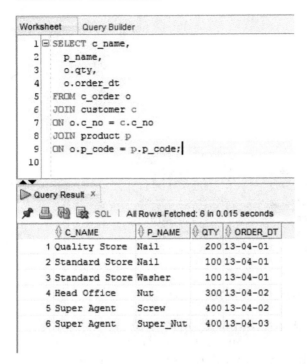

You can also apply WHERE conditions for selecting rows on a join query, as demonstrated in the following query. Now, only products with names that do not start with "Super" will be in the query output.

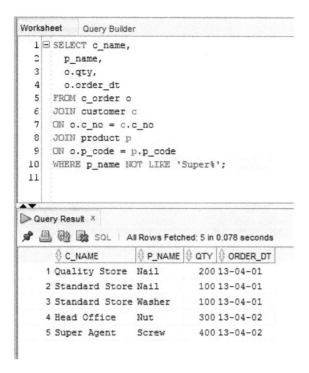

Joining on More than One Column

The preceding joins were on one column. Tables can also be joined on more than one column.

The syntax for a multicolumn join for two tables is as follows.

```
SELECT columns FROM table_1, table_2
WHERE table_1.column_1 = table_2.column_1
AND table_1.column_2 = table_2.column_2
...
AND table_1.column_n = table_2.column_n;
```

Here is an example of joining on two columns.

```
 1 □ SELECT o.c_no,
 2      o.p_code,
 3      o.order_dt,
 4      s.qty shipped_qty,
 5      s_dt,
 6      o.qty order_qty
 7   FROM shp s
 8   JOIN c_order o
 9   ON s.c_no     = o.c_no
10   AND s.p_code  = o.p_code
11   AND s.order_dt = o.order_dt;
12
```

Query Result ×

SQL | All Rows Fetched: 2 in 0.016 seconds

	C_NO	P_CODE	ORDER_DT	SHIPPED_QTY	S_DT	ORDER_QTY
1	10 1		13-04-01	100	13-04-05	100
2	10 2		13-04-01	100	13-04-05	100

No Foreign/Primary Key Relationship

The INV is a standalone table. But, somehow we know that C_ORDER table is related to INV table. Their common columns are INV's WAREHOUSE and P_CODE and C_ORDER's SOURCE and P_CODE. (SOURCE is the warehouse source from where the product on order has been allocated)

In a real-world environment, hopefully these common columns are documented in one way or another. Otherwise, you will have to investigate from perhaps some data of the potentially related tables and their columns. You can learn how to how to find out common columns (table relationship) by learning the techniques in Part II of this book.

So, the query to retrieve the source (warehouse) of an order is as follows.

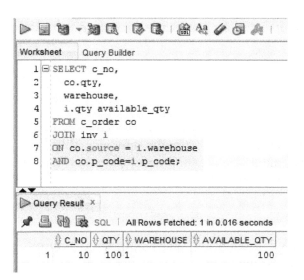

Outer Joins

All the joins I explained so far were inner joins. There is another type of join, the outer join. While an inner join query produces only related rows from the joined tables, an outer join query produces all rows from one table even when some of the rows do not have matching rows from the other table.

There are three subtypes of outer joins, LEFT, RIGHT, and FULL. The following points described each of these three types.

All rows from the table on the left of the left outer join will be in the output whether or not there are matching rows from the table on its right. The syntax for the left outer join is as follows.

```
SELECT columns
FROM table_1 LEFT OUTER JOIN table_2
ON table_1.column = table_2.column ... ;
```

All rows form the table on the right of the right outer join will be in the output whether or not there are matching rows from the table on its left. The syntax for the right outer join is as follows.

```
SELECT columns FROM table_1 RIGHT OUTER JOIN
table_2 ON table_1.column = table_2.column ...
;
```

The full outer join returns all rows from both tables whether or not there are matching rows from the opposite table. The syntax for the full outer join is as follows.

```
SELECT columns
FROM table_1 FULL OUTER JOIN table_2
ON table_1.column = table_2.column ... ;
```

Here is an example left outer join query. This query returns all rows from the c_order table.

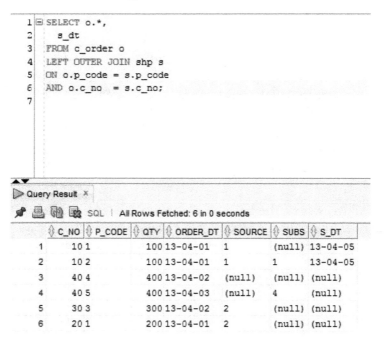

```
1 ⊟ SELECT o.*,
2       s_dt
3   FROM c_order o
4   LEFT OUTER JOIN shp s
5   ON o.p_code = s.p_code
6   AND o.c_no = s.c_no;
7
```

Query Result ✕

SQL | All Rows Fetched: 6 in 0 seconds

	C_NO	P_CODE	QTY	ORDER_DT	SOURCE	SUBS	S_DT
1	10	1	100	13-04-01	1	(null)	13-04-05
2	10	2	100	13-04-01	1	1	13-04-05
3	40	4	400	13-04-02	(null)	(null)	(null)
4	40	5	400	13-04-03	(null)	4	(null)
5	30	3	300	13-04-02	2	(null)	(null)
6	20	1	200	13-04-01	2	(null)	(null)

Note that the last two rows have no matching rows from the

shipment table and therefore their ship_dt column has NULL values.

Rows with NULL only

If you want to query only orders that have not been shipped at all, you have to put this "only" condition in the WHERE clause of your query (s_dt IS NULL) as in the following query.

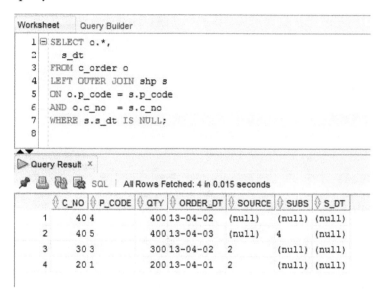

Full Outer Joins

To return orders that do not have shipments as well shipments that do not have orders, we need to write a query with the full outer join, like the one shown next.

```
Worksheet     Query Builder
1 ⊟ SELECT o.*, s.s_dt
2      FROM c_order o
3   FULL OUTER JOIN shp s
4   ON o.p_code = s.p_code
5   AND o.c_no  = s.c_no ;
6
```

▷ Query Result ×

🔖 🖨 ▣ ▣ SQL | All Rows Fetched: 6 in 0.031 seconds

	C_NO	P_CODE	QTY	ORDER_DT	SOURCE	SUBS	S_DT
1	10	1	100	13-04-01	1	(null)	13-04-05
2	10	2	100	13-04-01	1	1	13-04-05
3	20	1	200	13-04-01	2	(null)	(null)
4	30	3	300	13-04-02	2	(null)	(null)
5	40	4	400	13-04-02	(null)	(null)	(null)
6	40	5	400	13-04-03	(null)	4	(null)

Self-Joins

In our data model, the C_ORDER table has the SUBS column for the substitute of product in the order. We can actually have a different model, where the SUBS is on the PRODUCT table. In this case, the PRODUCT table, for example, has the Screw having SUBS = 5, while the others do not have any substitute.

	P_CODE	P_NAME	PRICE	LAUNCH_DT	SUBS
1		Nail	10	15-03-31	(null)
2		Washer	15	13-03-29	(null)
3		Nut	15	13-03-29	(null)
4		Screw	25	13-03-30	5
5		Super_Nut	30	13-03-30	(null)
6		New Nut	(null)	(null)	(null)

If you need to retrieve the product name of a substitute, you need a query that joins the product table to itself. This kind of join is called a self-join.

The syntax for the self-join is as follows.

```
SELECT columns
FROM table alias_1
JOIN table alias_2
ON alias_1.column_x = alias_2.column_y;
```

Note that *column_x* and *column_y* are columns in the same table.

Here is an example of self-join query.

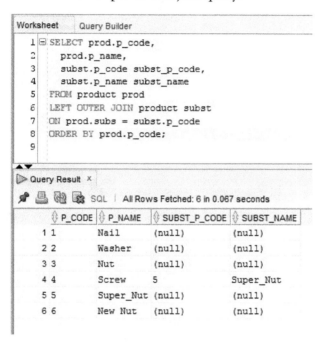

Natural Joins

If two tables have columns that share a name, you can naturally join the two tables on these columns. In a natural join, you do not need to specify the columns that the join should use.

The syntax for the natural join is this.

```
SELECT columns FROM table_1 NATURAL JOIN table_2 ...
    ;
```

The following is an example of natural join query, which implicitly joins the tables on their c_no columns.

```
SELECT * FROM c_order NATURAL JOIN customer;
```

	C_NO	P_CODE	QTY	ORDER_DT	SOURCE	SUBS	C_NAME		ADDRESS	CITY	PROV
1	10	1	100	13-04-01	1	(null)	Standard Store	10	University Ave	Toronto	ON
2	10	2	100	13-04-01	1	1	Standard Store	10	University Ave	Toronto	ON
3	20	1	200	13-04-01	2	(null)	Quality Store	20	Windham Street	Toronto	ON
4	30	3	300	13-04-02	2	(null)	Head Office	30	Burbank Dr	North York	ON
5	40	4	400	13-04-02	(null)	(null)	Super Agent	40	Palomino Ave	North York	ON
6	40	5	400	13-04-03	(null)	4	Super Agent	40	Palomino Ave	North York	ON

Natural Outer Joins

The natural join is also applicable to the outer join.

```
SELECT * FROM c_order NATURAL RIGHT JOIN customer;
```

	C_NO	P_CODE	QTY	ORDER_DT	SOURCE	SUBS	C_NAME		ADDRESS	CITY	PROV
1	10	1	100	13-04-01	1	(null)	Standard Store	10	University Ave	Toronto	ON
2	10	2	100	13-04-01	1	1	Standard Store	10	University Ave	Toronto	ON
3	20	1	200	13-04-01	2	(null)	Quality Store	20	Windham Street	Toronto	ON
4	30	3	300	13-04-02	2	(null)	Head Office	30	Burbank Dr	North York	ON
5	40	4	400	13-04-02	(null)	(null)	Super Agent	40	Palomino Ave	North York	ON
6	40	5	400	13-04-03	(null)	4	Super Agent	40	Palomino Ave	North York	ON

Mixing Natural Joins with Different Column Names

If you need to join on more than one column, and the second column pair does not share a name, you can specify the different column names in the WHERE clause as shown in the following example.

The query, in addition to the natural join on the same c_no column, joins the two tables on the two dates. It does not return any row as we don't have any order of a product with the same order date as the product's launch date.

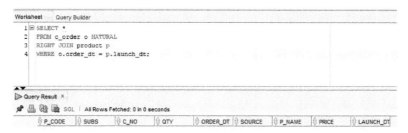

The USING Keyword

A natural join will use all columns with the same names from the joined tables. If you want your query to join on identically named columns use the USING keyword.

The syntax for joining two tables with USING is as follows.

```
SELECT columns
FROM table_1
JOIN table_2 USING (column);
```

Here is an example query.

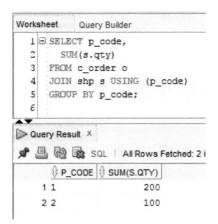

Chapter 7: Subqueries

A subquery is a query nested within another query. The containing query is called an outer query; the subquery is also known as the inner query.

This chapter discusses subqueries in detail.

Single-Row Subqueries

A single-row subquery is a subquery that returns a single value.

- A single-row subquery can be placed in the WHERE clause of an outer query.
- If more than one is returned, you will get an error message.
- The return value of the subquery is compared with a column of the outer query using one of the comparison operators.
- The column and subquery result do not have to be the same column, but they must have compatible data types.

The following query contains a single-row subquery.

- The inner query (printed in bold) returns the highest sale price recorded for a product.
- The outer query returns all products from the product table that have that highest price (30.00), the Super_Nut and Newer Nut products.

```
Worksheet    Query Builder
  1 ⊟ SELECT * FROM product
  2   WHERE price =
  3 ⊟   (SELECT MAX(price)
  4     FROM product p
  5     INNER JOIN c_order o
  6     ON p.p_code = o.p_code
  7     );
  8
```

Script Output × ▷ Query Result ×

📌 🖨 🔁 📇 SQL | All Rows Fetched: 1 in 0.031 seconds

P_CODE	P_NAME	PRICE	LAUNCH_DT	S_CODE
1 5	Super_Nut	30	13-03-30	(null)

Multiple-Row Subqueries

A subquery that returns more than one value is called a multiple-row subquery.

- This type of subquery also occurs in the WHERE clause of an outer query
- Instead of using a comparison operator, you use IN or NOT IN.

Here is an example.

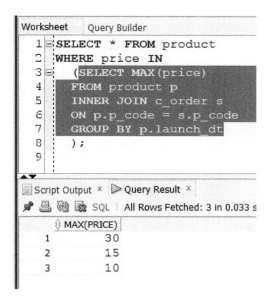

The outer query output will be as follows.

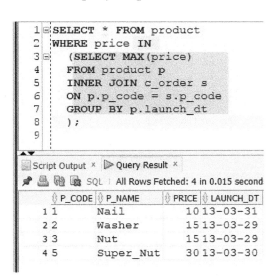

ALL and ANY Operators

In addition to IN and NOT IN, you can also use the ALL and ANY operators in a multiple-row subquery.

- With ALL or ANY you use a comparison operator.
- For instance, in the following query ALL compares the price to all output rows of the subquery result.
- The query output will consist of only rows whose price is greater or equal to all the values returned by the subquery, effectively to the highest price (30)

```
1  SELECT *
2  FROM product
3  WHERE price >= ALL
4    (SELECT MAX(price)
5    FROM product p
6    INNER JOIN c_order o
7    ON o.p_code  = o.p_code
8    WHERE price IS NOT NULL
9    GROUP BY p.launch_dt
10   )
11 ORDER BY p_code;
12
```

Script Output × ▷ Query Result ×

📌 🖨 ⏰ 📇 SQL | All Rows Fetched: 1 in 0.016 second:

P_CODE	P_NAME	PRICE	LAUNCH_DT
1 5	Super_Nut	30	13-03-30

Nested Subqueries

A subquery can contain another query, making it a query with multiple nested subqueries, such as in the following example.

```
1  SELECT c_name,c_no
2  FROM customer
3  WHERE c_no IN
4    (SELECT c_no
5     FROM c_order
6     WHERE p_code IN
7       (SELECT p_code FROM product WHERE p_name NOT LIKE '%Nut%'
8       )
9    );
10
```

Script Output × ▷ Query Result ×

📌 🖴 📖 📑 SQL | All Rows Fetched: 3 in 0.062 seconds

	C_NAME	C_NO
1	Standard Store	10
2	Quality Store	20
3	Super Agent	40

Correlated Subqueries

All the preceding subqueries are independent of their outer queries. A subquery can also be related to its outer query, where one or more column from the outer query table is (are) related to the column(s) of the subquery table in the WHERE clause of the subquery.

▪ This type of subquery is called the correlated subquery.

   The following query contains a correlated subquery
▪ The subquery returns only customers who have not ordered any product whose name contains 'Nut'.
▪ The c_no column of the outer query table, customer, is related to the c_no column of the c_order table of the subquery.

```
 1 ⊟ SELECT c_name, c_no FROM customer
 2   WHERE c_no IN
 3 ⊟   (SELECT c_no
 4     FROM c_order o
 5     JOIN product p
 6     ON o.p_code = p.p_code
 7     WHERE p_name NOT LIKE '%Nut%'
 8     AND customer.c_no = o.c_no
 9     );
10
```

Script Output × ▷ Query Result ×

SQL | All Rows Fetched: 3 in 0.016 seconds

C_NAME	C_NO
1 Standard Store	10
2 Quality Store	20
3 Super Agent	40

Factoring

Using a WITH clause you can factor out a subquery placing it above the main SELECT, and give it a name.

- You can then use it in the main query by referring its name as if it is a table.
- The syntax of the WITH clause is as follows.

```
WITH sub_query_name AS (subquery)
SELECT ...
    );
```

The following query has the WITH factoring.

```
1  WITH max_price AS
2      (SELECT MAX(price)
3      FROM product p
4      INNER JOIN c_order o
5      ON p.p_code = o.p_code
6      )
7  SELECT * FROM product WHERE price =
8      (SELECT * FROM max_price
9      );
10
```

Script Output × ▷ Query Result ×

📌 🖨 🔁 📑 SQL | All Rows Fetched: 1 in 0.015 seconds

MAX(PRICE)
1   30

You can see that our main query is cleaner; the subquery factoring helps its clarity.

The factored subquery in the following query has more benefits as it is used more than once (i.e. twice) in the main query.

The factored subquery output is the maximum price by month.

Worksheet   Query Builder

```
1  WITH max_price AS
2      (SELECT MAX(price) max_price, extract(MONTH FROM p.launch_dt) launch_mth
3      FROM product p
4      WHERE price IS NOT NULL
5      GROUP BY extract(MONTH FROM p.launch_dt)
6      )
7  SELECT DISTINCT
8      (SELECT max_price FROM max_price WHERE launch_mth < 5
9      ) "Before May",
10      (SELECT max_price FROM max_price WHERE launch_mth >= 5
11      ) "May or After"
12  FROM product;
13
```

Script Output × ▷ Query Result ×

📌 🖨 🔁 📑 SQL | All Rows Fetched: 1 in 0.015 seconds

MAX_PRICE	LAUNCH_MTH
1 30	3

And the query output is:

```
Worksheet   Query Builder
 1  WITH max_price AS
 2    (SELECT MAX(price) max_price, extract(MONTH FROM p.launch_dt) launch_mth
 3     FROM product p
 4     WHERE price IS NOT NULL
 5     GROUP BY extract(MONTH FROM p.launch_dt)
 6    )
 7  SELECT DISTINCT
 8    (SELECT max_price FROM max_price WHERE launch_mth < 5
 9    ) "Before May",
10    (SELECT max_price FROM max_price WHERE launch_mth >= 5
11    ) "May or After"
12  FROM product;
13
```

Script Output × ▷ Query Result ×

📌 🖥 🐵 🐵 SQL | All Rows Fetched: 1 in 0.016 seconds

Before May	May or After
30	(null)

(row 1)

Chapter 8: Compound Queries

You can combine the results of two or more SELECT statements using the four set operators: UNION ALL, UNION, INTERSECT, and MINUS.

- The number of output columns from every statement must be the same and the corresponding columns must have identical or compatible data types.
- The resulting compound query is just one SELECT statement.

UNION ALL

The UNION ALL operator combines the output all rows from its queries.

In the following example the UNION ALL combines all output rows from the two SELECT statements.

I added the 'FIRST QUERY' and 'SECOND_QUERY' literals (3rd output column) in the first and second SELECT statements, respectively. They help identify the query a row comes from.

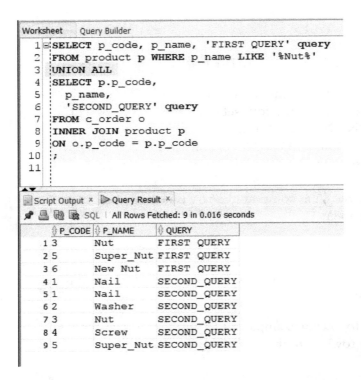

You can apply ORDER BY clause, for example, by the p_code column.

- You can only have on ORDER BY and it must be at the end of the whole query.

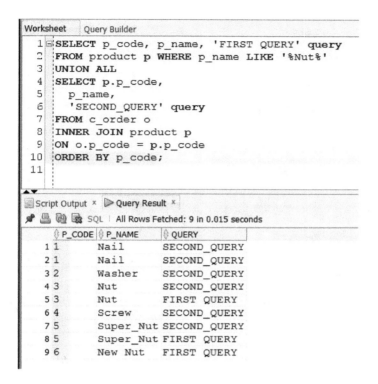

UNION

While UNION ALL returns all rows, UNION will return duplicate rows **once only**.

Here is an example query that has a UNION.

```
Worksheet    Query Builder
  1 ⊟ SELECT p_code,
  2 ┊    p_name
  3 ┊ FROM product p
  4 ┊ WHERE p_name LIKE '%Nut%'
  5 ┊ UNION
  6 ┊ SELECT p.p_code,
  7 ┊    p_name
  8 ┊ FROM c_order o
  9 ┊ INNER JOIN product p
 10 ┊ ON o.p_code = p.p_code
 11 ┊ ORDER BY p_code;
 12 ┊
```

Script Output × ▷ Query Result ×

📌 🖥 🖼 📑 SQL | All Rows Fetched: 6 in 0.016 s

P_CODE	P_NAME
1 1	Nail
2 2	Washer
3 3	Nut
4 4	Screw
5 5	Super_Nut
6 6	New Nut

INTERSECT

When you combine two or more queries with the INTERSECT operator, the output will be rows commonly returned by to all participating SELECT statements. In other words, only if a row is returned by all the SELECT statements will the row be included in the final result.

```
Worksheet    Query Builder
  1 ⊟ SELECT p_code,
  2      p_name
  3   FROM product p
  4   WHERE p_name LIKE '%Nut%'
  5   INTERSECT
  6   SELECT p.p_code,
  7      p_name
  8   FROM c_order o
  9   INNER JOIN product p
 10   ON o.p_code = p.p_code
 11   ORDER BY p_code;
 12
```

Script Output ×   ▷ Query Result ×

🖈 🖳 🕸 🖳 SQL | All Rows Fetched: 2 in 0.016 se

P_CODE	P_NAME
1 3	Nut
2 5	Super_Nut

MINUS

When you combine two SELECT statements using the MINUS operator, the final output will be rows from the first query that are not returned by the second query; any rows that are the same from the two queries are not in the output.

[86]

```
Worksheet    Query Builder
  1 ⊟SELECT p_code,
  2  :   p_name
  3  :FROM product p
  4  :WHERE p_name LIKE '%Nut%'
  5  :MINUS
  6  :SELECT p.p_code,
  7  :   p_name
  8  :FROM c_order o
  9  :INNER JOIN product p
 10  :ON o.p_code = p.p_code
 11  :ORDER BY p_code;
 12  :
```

Script Output × ▷ Query Result ×

📌 🖨 🔊 🔊 SQL | All Rows Fetched: 1 in 0.016 sec

P_CODE	P_NAME
1 6	New Nut

Chapter 9: Regular Expression

A regular expression is a sequence of characters that describes a pattern of text. The pattern is used to search for its occurrence in a string-type column of a table.

Regular expression is a big topic. This chapter will only cover only the basic.

Searching without Regular Expression

You have learned query that searches a string on exact match.

Assuming the customer table has the following columns and rows.

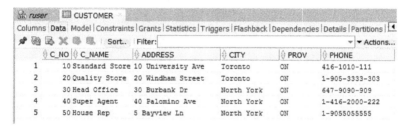

The following is an example query that searches string on exact match.

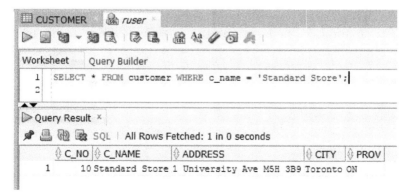

You also learned by using LIKE you don't need to be exact in the WHERE condition, that is approximate search.

The query will return all customers having the *Store* search word anywhere in their names.

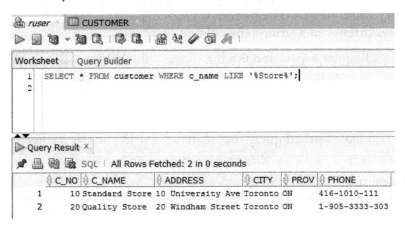

Pattern

A complete phone number stored in the table including its international code is expected to have the following pattern: i-aaa-nnnn-nnn; where i is the international code, aaa is the area code, the four n's and the three n's form the phone number, and these four parts must be separated by hyphen.

What if we would like to find the phone numbers that do not have a dash between the two parts of the seven digit phone number (the last three and its previous four numbers)?

The following query solves the question.

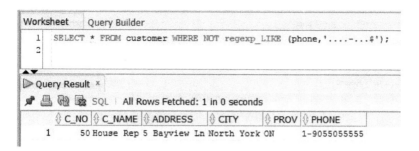

The above query uses the regular expression function, REGEXP_LIKE that has the following syntax.

REGEXP_LIKE(*searched_string*,'*pattern*');

Pattern Format

The pattern '....-...' in Listing 10.3 consists of . and $ regular expression metacharacters, and the – character which is not a metacharacter.

Pattern is Searched Anywhere

The pattern is searched anywhere in the searched_string, i.e. its effect is the same that in the LIKE with the surrounding pair of $. The following two queries produce the same output.

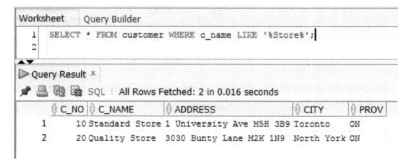

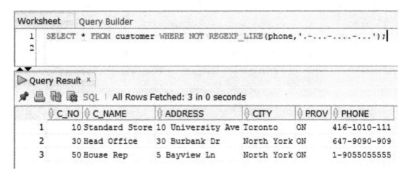

Using Meta Characters

You will next learn some of the other meta characters in the next sections.

. is for any one character

The . in a pattern represents any one character. You have seen the use of the . previously. Here's another query using the .

Though they are inside the pattern, the dashes (–) are normal characters (it is not a metacharacter).

Note that you cannot use the . to search for NULL.

| the Or

The | meta character is effectively an OR operator. The following query uses the | operator to find customers whose address has u or U.

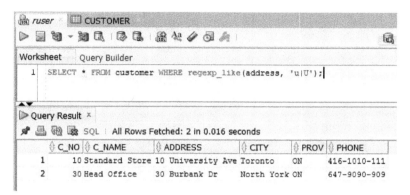

Quantifier

You can use the {m} meta character to avoid repeating a meta character. m is the number of repetition (count).

Here is an example query that uses the quantifier.

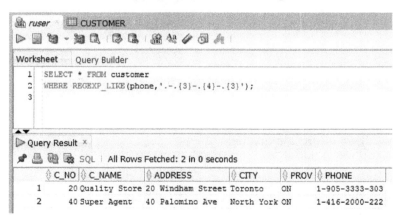

You can also apply the {m} to normal character, such as in the following query which searches for any address having two a's in sequence.

The query has no output row as the customer table has no such address.

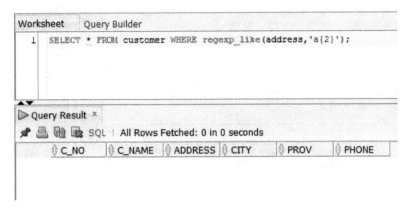

The {m} quantifier has two variations. {m,} means m or more, while {m,n) means m and more but up to n.

There are three additional quantifiers:

+ (plus sign) is for one or more (at least one)

? (question mark) for zero or one (maximum one)

* (asterisk) for zero or more (optional)

The following query is an example regular expression query using the +. It searches for any address that has an **i** followed by one or more **n**.

Two addresses qualify:

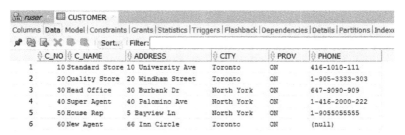

() Defining Sub Expression

Anything inside () is treated as one pattern, so if you want to apply the + to **"in"** as a pattern, then put them in parenthesis as in the following query. This query searches for addresses that have in once or more. (The + means one or more)

Assuming we have a new customer Super Agent residing on 66 Inn Circle as seen below.

The following two queries demonstrates the effect of with the () and without. The ? means zero or more. Hence the nn is optional.

In the first query, address with i will match as well address with inn. The second query is without () only addresses having in or inn will match as the in is mandatory.

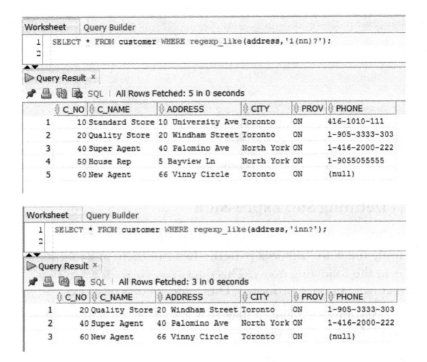

[...] for Matching List

The six characters Canadian postal-code that has an ANA NAN pattern where A is Alpha in uppercase and N is numeric with a space in between the two parts. We can use the pattern, [A-Z][1-9][A-Z] [1-9][A-Z][1-9], as shown in Listing 10.12, to search for correctly-patterned postal code, where A – Z means A, B, C, …, the alphabets in uppercase; and [1-9] means the nine numerical digits (0 is not in the list).

Assuming the addresses has the following postal codes of which only two postal codes have the correct pattern.

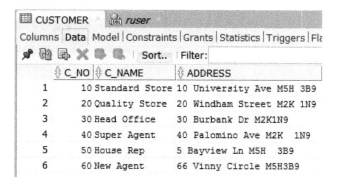

The next query shows the use of regular expression pattern to search for addresses with the correct pattern.

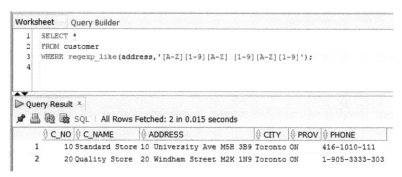

Chapter 10: Query as Database View

A view is effectively a predefined query.

- When you use a view the predefined query is executed.
- The query output is available just like if the query is executed outside of the view.
  - ○ Hence we can regard a view as a table, though it does not store any data.
  - ○ The data comes from the base tables retrieved by the predefined query.
- A view is a great way to wrap a complex query.

Creating View

You create a view using the CREATE VIEW statement, which has the following syntax.

```
CREATE VIEW view_name (columns) AS SELECT ... ;
```

The SELECT statement at the end of the CREATE VIEW statement is the predefined query. When you use a view its predefined query is executed.

A view is a database object created and stored in the database.
- As R users you may not be allowed to create views in the database.
- Discuss your need with the system/application owner

An example view

The following statement create a view named nut_product wrapping the example 'minus' query from the previous chapter.
- The predefined query is in bold.

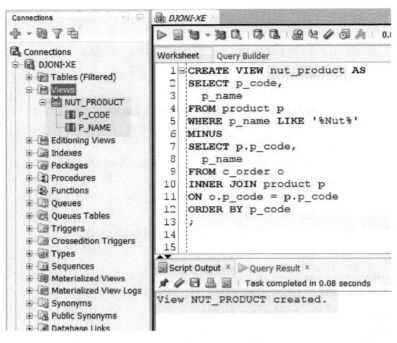

The nut_product view can now be used just as you would any database table. For example, the following statement displays all data of the view.

```
SELECT * FROM nut_product;
```

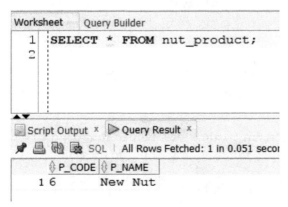

View in R

R can simply regard view as a table and uses dbReadTable method to transparently run the query and load the rows returned by the query.

Here is an example.

- SQL in the database is not case sensitive, but R is. So, the name of the view in R should be as you see in the SQL Developer, which in our case here is in uppercases.

```
> library('ROracle')
> drv <- dbDriver("Oracle")
> con <- dbConnect(drv, "djoni", "pw", "host:1521/xe")
>
> v <- dbReadTable(con,"NUT_PRODUCT")
>
> class(v)
[1] "data.frame"
>
> v
   P_CODE   P_NAME
1       6 New Nut
>
```

Available views

To see available views on the GUI, expand the Views folder.

When you click a view, you will see its columns and its data on the Data tab.

You can see the query (SQL statement) wrapped in the view on the SQL tab.

```
1
2   CREATE OR REPLACE FORCE VIEW "DJONI"."CUSTOMER_ORDER" ("C_NAME", "P_NAME", "PRICE", "QTY", "ORDER_DATE") AS
3   SELECT C_NAME, P_NAME,
4   PRICE, QTY,
5   TO_CHAR(ORDER_DT, 'DD-MON-YYYY') ORDER_DATE
6 FROM PRODUCT p
7 JOIN C_ORDER co
8 ON p.P_CODE = co.P_CODE
9 JOIN CUSTOMER c
10 ON c.C_NO = co.C_NO;
11
```

Sharing/Securing View

When you create a view, you own it. A GRANT statement permits other users to use the view, at the same time you control its access securing the view.

The GRANT statement has the following syntax.

```
GRANT SELECT
ON view_name
TO user;
```

An example would be:

```
GRANT
SELECT ON nut_product TO user1;
```

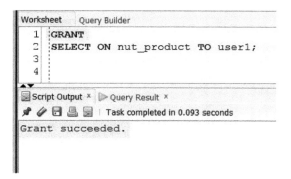

Note that in your real-world environment, as an R user, you might not have the privilege to issue a grant. In this case, ask for help from your database administrator.

Part II: Identifying and Exploring Data

As mentioned at the beginning of Part I, to write a query (SELECT statement) you must know the names of the table and columns that stores the data you want to retrieve the data, and if necessary also the common columns to join tables.

In the chapters of this part (Part II), you will learn to use the GUI facilities of SQL Developer to identify table, column, table relationship and the common columns.

Part I consist of four chapters in which we will:
- Set up database connection.
- Review how data is stored in SQL database.
- Identify tables and columns, and relationship of tables.
- Explore data to confirm the tables and columns actually contain the data we need.

Steps to Identify Columns and Tables

At the high-level, identifying tables and columns that store the data consists three steps.

1. Gathering initial information

Before identifying the tables and columns, you need to gather initial information from the SME's (Subject Matter Expert).
- SME can be the business people, IT community, and your R user colleagues.
- You should gather only information related to the data you need for your R.

The information includes:
- **Sample data from the real data, with the exact spelling as stored in the database. If you have no**

**change to getting nothing else (none of the next three
items below), you must have the sample data.**

- o Note that sample data here can be just a few (not the
  sample data as used for statistical purpose)
- Standard or convention in data names and abbreviations.
- Data model, such as ERD (Entity Relationship Diagram).
  The ERD is still useful even if it uses different style and
  notation from the SQL Developer's we use in this book.
- Business glossary including the terminologies commonly
  used in the business. This information is useful not only
  the terminologies, but also a source of knowledge of their
  definitions and meanings.

The SME's might show you the information right on the
computer or in print.

2. Identifying column and table by their names

Equipped with the above information, we will then use the
GUI of SQL Developer to identify exactly the columns and
their tables that stores the data we are after.

Metadata

The information we look up in this and next steps (Step1 and
2) are stored in and maintained by the database system. The
storage, which contains much more data than about tables
and columns, is called metadata.

But, we will only use the metadata for our specific
purpose, i.e. looking up the information about tables and
columns, which we need to write SQL queries. We will look
up this specific metadata using the SQL Developer's GUI
facilities provided for the purpose.

3. Confirming data

Having the potential columns and tables by names, we are now confirming they store the correct data we are after.

In particular, we will verify the existence of the sample data we gather in step 1.

Again, we use the SQL Developer facilities to do this job.

In the next chapters we will elaborate step 2 and 3. But first, we need to do two kinds of preparation:
- Setting database connection
- Understanding how data is stored in a database.

Chapter 11: Database Connection

To identify tables and columns, we need to have database connection in our SQL Developer.

You might be in one of the following three situations.

- Your IT support might have set the database connection you need. The connection is available for your immediate use.
- You might have been given the connection as an xml file. You need to import it into your SQL Developer.
- You need to set up the connection yourself.

Connection is Available

When you already have the database connection you should see its name, e.g. ruser as shown below.

A connection is secured by a password. If it is not imbedded in the connection you should be given the password.

Verify you can connect as follows.

- Double click the connection.

■ If the password is not stored in the connection, you will be prompted to enter.

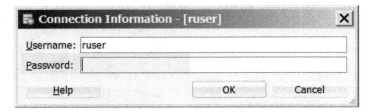

Importing Connection

If you are given the connection, an xml file, you will need to install it.

■ Import the xml file by right-clicking the Connections > Import Connections.

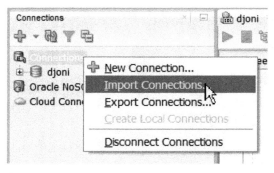

■ Locate the xml file where it is stored; then, click the Next button.

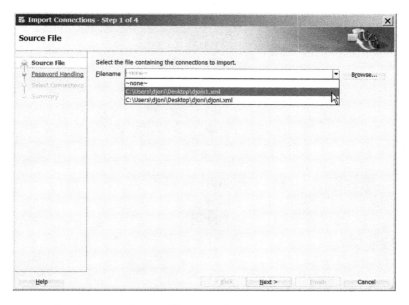

Next, the Password Handling section will show up.

You need the password from whoever gave you the connection xml. You can either type in the password on the Encryption Key field or select "Remove … ".

If choose to remove, you will have to type in the password every time you use the connection. In a way it's safer—anyone happens to use your SQL Developer must know the password.

Then, click the Next button.

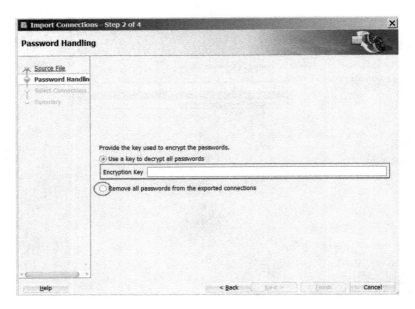

The xml might contain more than one connection.

■ Select the one(s) you need, and then click the Finish button.

■ The connection you are importing should be in the list.

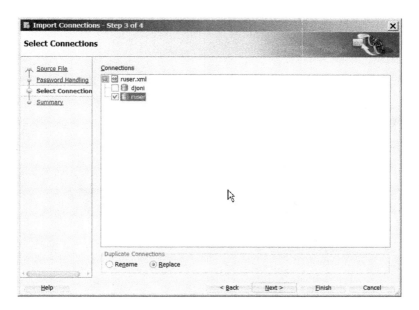

To make sure it is a good connection, test it.
- Double click the connection.
- If the password is not stored in the connection, you will be prompted to enter.

Creating a New Connection

To create a connection, you need the following five pieces of info from your system or database administrator, or your IT support.
- Username and its password.
- Hostname, port number, and SID of the database.

If you are able to connect to the database from R, then you already have this information.
- This is the "user_name, password, host_name:port_number/database_name" parameter of the dbConnect. In the following R command for example, this is the djoni, pasword, localhost:1521/xe, respectively, written in bold in the following R command.

```
> con <- dbConnect(drv, "djoni", "password",
"localhost:1521/xe")
```

Having the above info you can now create the connection.

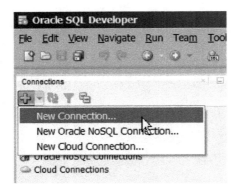

Type in the connection name you of your choice, and enter the five pieces of info.

Decide to save the password along with the connection by checking the box or not.

- If you don't, you will be prompted every time you open the connection to access the database.

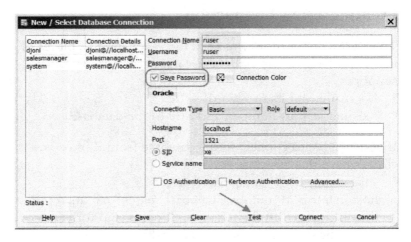

Test the connection by clicking the Test button.

- If it's good, you should see Success on the Status (bottom left hand corner)

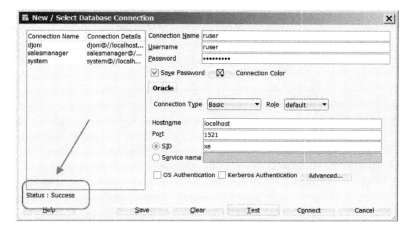

Chapter 12: Identifying Tables and Columns

It would be best if you are able to get the exact names of table and column where the data you are after is stored, and sample data stored in the column. The only thing left for you to do is verifying that the column contains the sample data.

In other cases you might only get the table name or only approximate names of table or column, but in any these other cases, you should have sample data.

The following sections show you how using the GUI of SQL Developer you can locate the table, column and sample data.

Listing Tables

Start the SQL Developer, and connect to the database by clicking the + on the connection. The ruser folder will be expanded.

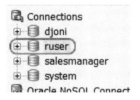

The subfolders will be shown.

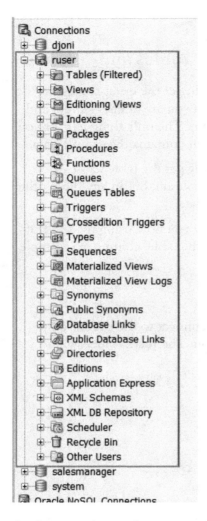

As the ruser is not the owner of the tables we cannot see the tables under the ruser. The owner is salesmanager, so expand the Other Users folder (the last in the list) and then expand the salesmanager folder and then its Tables folder.

Note that in your real-world environment you should know the schema owner of the tables, usually you ask the database administrator.

Locate the table from the table list, and click the table you were told having the sample data; let's say, CUSTOMER.

Note: the table is listed sorted alphabetically ascending A to Z downward.

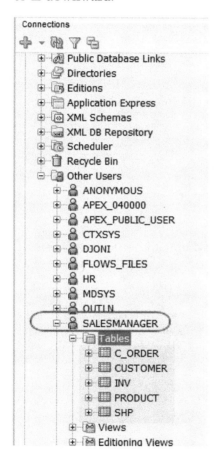

Open the Data tab, and locate the columns you were told having the sample data. For example, Head Office in C_NAME column and its address 10 University Ave in ADDRESS column.

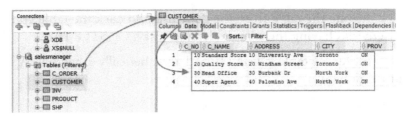

Filtering Data

If the table has lots of data, you might have difficulty locating the sample data. If so, then use the Filter facility.

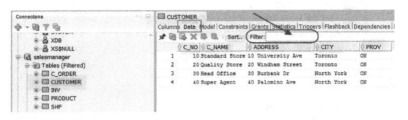

On the Filter enter (type) the column and its sample data as shown, then press Enter key.

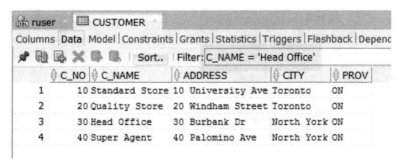

If Head Office exists in the C_NAME column, the row(s) will be displayed.

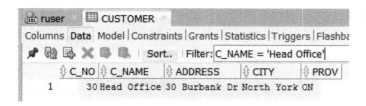

Filtering Tables

If you have many tables, you might have difficulty locating the table you were told having the sample data. You can narrow down some specific tables at a time.

Right-click the Tables folder, then select "Apply Filter".

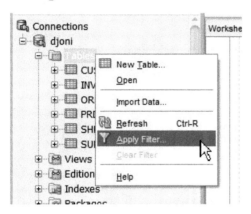

On the Filter window, enter your filter criteria.

- In the example below, my filter is: only show tables that have O anywhere in the name.
- The % means any number of any characters. You can place a % anywhere: at the beginning, end or anywhere in the middle of the word that is part of the table/column name.

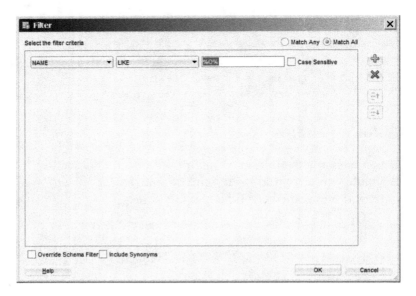

The tables shown will be SHP and SUP only.

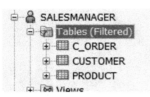

The filter criteria have some additional settings.

- Filter is case sensitive if you check the "Case Sensitive" box.
- You can have more than one line of filter. You add a new line by clicking the green +; remove a line by clicking the red X.
- If you have multiple lines, you can specify if all should be satisfied or just any one line.

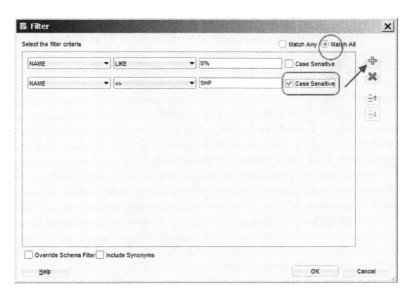

Clearing Filter

You can clear a filter b right-clicking the Tables folder and then select "Clear Filter".

You might have noticed that in addition to tables, the connection also shows quite some other objects not relevant to our purpose. These other objects clutter our view sometimes making it difficult to identify our target tables.

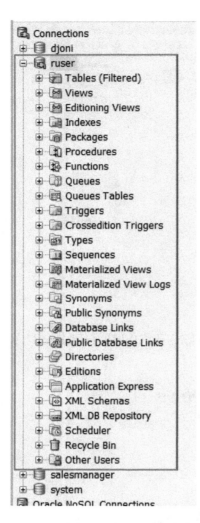

To see tables **only**, right-click the connection, then select Schema Browser.

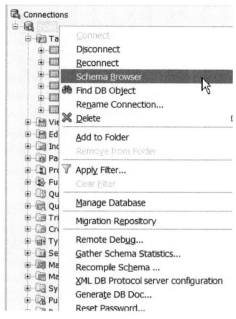

Select our salesmanager schema from the drop down.

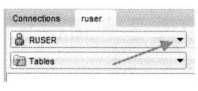

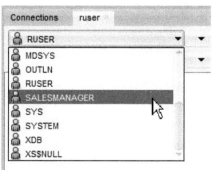

And select Tables from the object drop-down. Only tables will be listed, no other objects in the list, helping us in identifying our target tables.

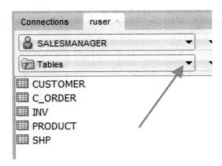

Search by Name

SQL Developer has a feature to search object by name (table is one such an object), which is most useful if the database has lots of tables and you are not sure the names of tables and columns that have the data you are after.

Your search can include columns in addition to table.

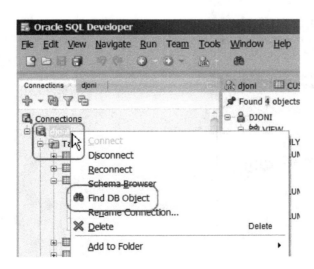

The "Find Database Object" panel will be available.

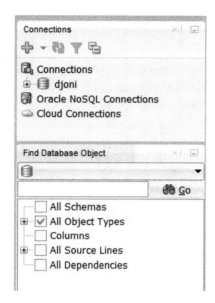

You can set an exact search or approximate search.

- In an exact search, you set the search word exactly the name of the object you want to find, QTY in the following example. To start the search, click the Go button.

The search result will be as shown below. The table and column that satisfy the QTY criteria has their names highlighted in green on their QTY characters.

- The QTY column in INV and ORD tables and MONTHLY_ORDER view. (You will in a later chapter learn how create this view)

- If you want to find all tables and columns that have OR in their names, your setting will be an approximate search as shown. (You can learn more about approximate search in the LIKE section of Chapter 2)
  - On the search field type in %OR%. The % means any number of any characters. The search is sort of saying: Approximately OR, or something like OR.
  - Check TABLES and Columns.

To start the search, click the Go button.

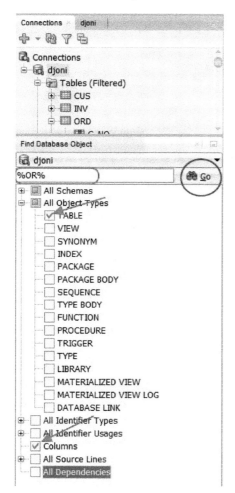

The search result will be as shown below. The table and column that satisfy the %OR% criteria has their names highlighted in green on their OR characters.

- The ORDER_DATE column in the MONTHLY_ORDER view. In the view itself the OR is not highlighted, as we did not select VIEW as an object to search in the setting.

- The ORDER_DT column in ORD and SHP table.
- And lastly, the ORD table.

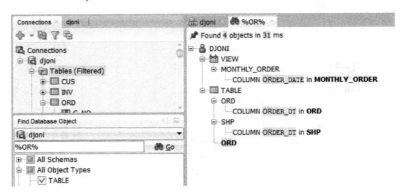

If you cannot find the table, column or sample data, you might want to try locating the data on another column:
- Based on similarity of name, or the data type (string, numeric, date)
- You might spot visually listed on the screen on the other column.

Otherwise you have to go back to the person who gave you the sample data and ask for clarification as you can't the sample data anywhere in the database.

Identifying Relationships

If you need to join two tables in your query, you must identify the column names that relate the tables.

SQL Developer provides a facility to generate ERD. The diagram nicely visualizes the relationships of tables and the common columns.

If select a table (e.g. C_ORDER) and then the Model tab, an ERD (Entity Relationship Diagram) will be displayed. The selected table will be the central of the diagram, its box is red.

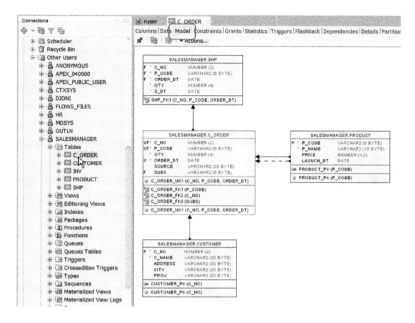

Reading ERD

Here's how you read the ERD.

Box is Table

First, a box represents a table.
- The red box is the central table (the table being opened), the related tables in blue.
- The name of table is on the top section of the box.
- Columns and their data types are listed in the second section.
  - A red * indicates not null able, the data is mandatory.
  - P is primary key, F is foreign key.
  - U (not available in the ERD above) is unique key. PRD has a U.
- Primary and Unique key, if any, is in the third.
- Foreign key(s), if any, is in the fourth.
- The last section lists indexes, if any. Appendix C has more about index.

Next, the arrows.

- An arrow represents a relationship between two tables.
- The direction of the arrow is from the parent to the child table (you can reverse the direction if you want to)
- The relationship is on the parent's primary key to the child's foreign key. For example, the primary key CUSTOMER_PK of the CUSTOMER parent table relates this table to foreign key C_ORDER_FK1 of the ORD child table.
- When you join the two tables the join condition is on the columns of the primary/foreign key:
  - ```
    SELECT * FROM customer JOIN ord ON
    customer.C_NO = c_ord.C_NO
    ```
    ```

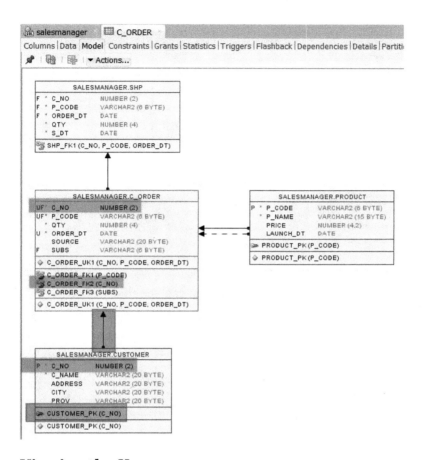

Viewing the Keys

When you double-click a table, its properties window will be shown.

The following is for example, the properties of the CUSTOMER table. You can see its columns by selecting Columns. The PK and FK check boxes indicate if a column is part of the table's primary and foreign key.

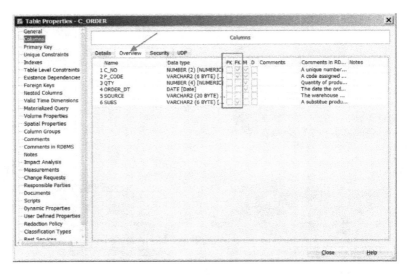

When you select Primary Key, you can see that C_NO is indeed the primary key column.

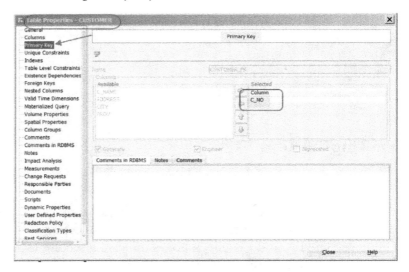

When you select Foreign Key or Unique Keys, you won't see any column assigned to any of the keys, as the CUSTOMER table does not have either foreign or unique key.

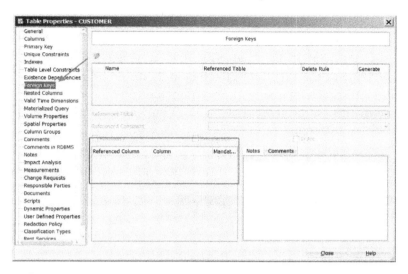

When you double-click C_ORDER table, and select Primary Key, you won't see anything as this table does not have any primary key. It does have a unique key, named C_ORDER_UK1, and that three columns form the unique key.

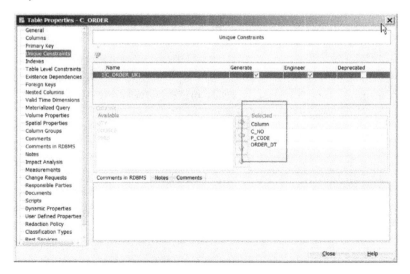

When you select Foreign Keys, you will see the table's foreign key(s), three in the case of this table (C_ORDER). The first one, C_ORDER_FK1, which is P_CODE column, relates the table to the PRODUCT table on its Referenced Column P_CODE. The name of the column and referenced column happen to be the same, P_CODE. You will see in a bit where they are different.

Notice that the C_ORDER's P_CODE column is checked mandatory (there must be a product on an order)

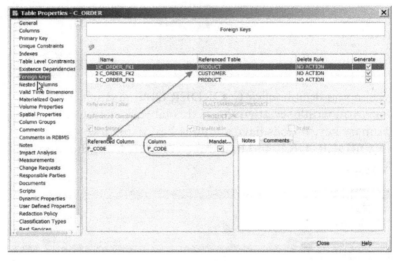

You might have noticed earlier on the Overview of Columns that SUBS column is a foreign key.

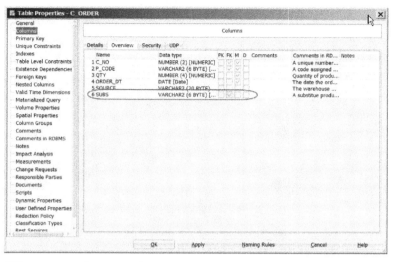

When you select Foreign Keys and C_ORDER_FK3, you will see that this foreign key's SUBS column relates the table to PRODUCT table on the P_CODE column, an example where the column and its referenced column have different names.

Notice also that the SUBS column is not mandatory (there can be no substitute product for a product being ordered)

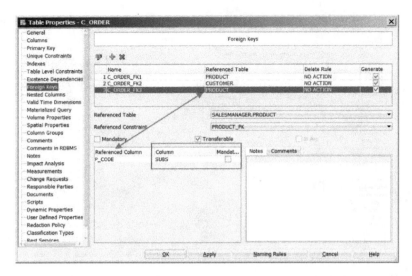

Having the details of the columns of the table relationship you are ready to join them on the query. (You will learn about join later in Chapter 9)

```
SELECT * FROM c_order JOIN product ON
c_order.subs = product.p_code;
```

As the subs column is not mandatory, and if we still want to see the order rows, we should apply an outer join.

```
SELECT * FROM c_order LEFT OUTER JOIN product
ON c_order.subs = product.p_code;
```

Including Other Tables

If you want to see other tables related to the non-central table, right-click the table, and then select the "Show Parent and Child Tables".

In the following example, the central table is SHP. We want to show other tables related to C_ORDER.

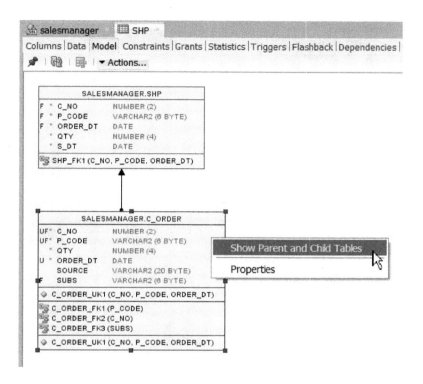

The related tables (PRODUCT and CUSTOMER) will added on the ERD.

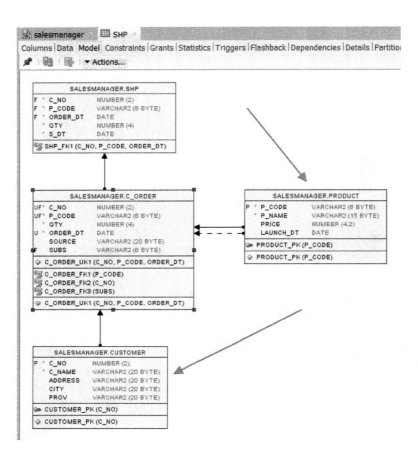

Chapter 13: Viewing the Data

So far, you have identified table, columns, and table relationships. To make sure the column has the data you are looking for you have to look at the data.

To view the data (rows) of a table, click the data tab of the table.

- In the following example, the rows of the CUSTOMER table are shown.

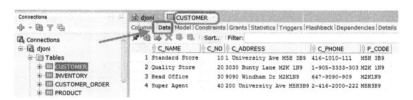

Sorting Rows

You can sort the rows by clicking the Sort button.

- Select the columns from the list on left that you want to be the sort columns, and click the > arrow. You can remove a sort column(s) from the right by clicking the < arrow. The >> and << move all columns on the left and all columns on the right, respectively.
- For each sort column, select its sort direction, Ascending or Descending.
- Also, if Null should be listed first or last.
- The order of the sort column is significant. You can move a column up or down using the ordering arrow.

When you are satisfied with the setting, click the OK button.

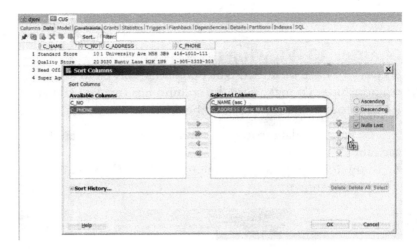

The rows will be sorted according to your sort setting.

- The sort column heading has the sign of sort direction and the order (number) of the sort column. For example, C_NAME is sort column number 1 and its direction is ascending.

^{1} C_NAME	C_NO	^{2} C_ADDRESS	C_PHONE
1 Head Office	30 9090 Windham Dr M2K1N9		647-9090-909
2 Quality Store	20 3030 Bunty Lane M2K 1N9		1-905-3333-303
3 Standard Store	10 1 University Ave M5H 3B9		416-1010-111
4 Super Agent	40 200 University Ave M5H3B9		2-416-2000-222

Viewing a Record

If the table has many columns, some of them on the right end might not be viewable on your screen.

On the Data tab, right-click the row you want to view its record.

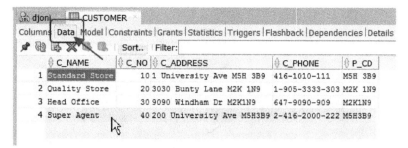

Select "Single Record View".

The record of the row you were right-clicking is shown on its own window.

- Use the arrows to move to the first, previous, next or the last record.
- In your real-world environment, just in case the user you use has the permission to update data, and you are not sure if you are allowed to actually update any data, don't click any of the pen icons.

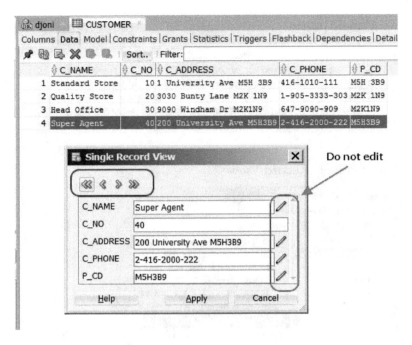

Viewing Specific Rows

If a table has lots of row, it would be challenging to look for some specific data.

Fortunately, you can select (search) rows to be displayed by setting filter criteria. The following screen show a simple filter C_NAME = 'Head Office'.

The Filter

The filter is actually the same as the condition of a WHERE clause, which you learn in Part I.

You can use, for example, the = <> > <, also IN and BETWEEN; and also the approximation using LIKE and

NOT LIKE, and REGEXP_LIKE, and even subquery, which you have/can learn in Part I.

An example using the REGEXP_LIKE and subquery is as follows.

When you press Enter, you will get the following result.

Appendix A: Installing DB Express and SQL Developer

The Appendix guides you to get and install the Oracle Data Base Express Edition and SQL Developer.

Oracle Database Express Edition

Go to
http://www.oracle.com/technetwork/indexes/downloads/index.html

Locate and download the Windows version of the Oracle Database Express Edition (XE). You will be requested to accept the license agreement. If you don't have one, create an account; it's free.

Unzip the downloaded file to a folder in your local drive, and then, double-click the setup.exe file.

You will see the Welcome window.

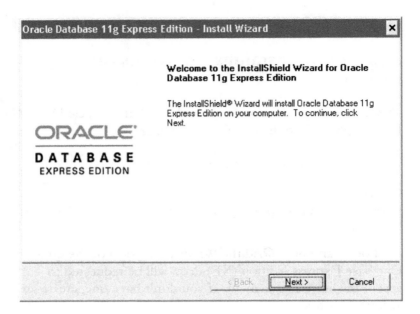

Click the Next> button, accept the agreement on the License Agreement window, and then click the Next> button again.

The next window is the "Choose Destination Location" window.

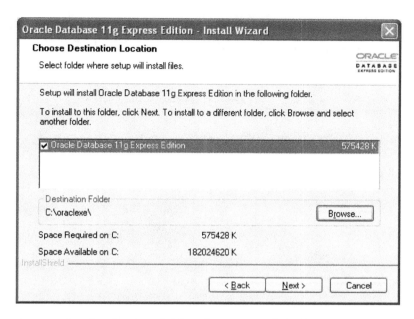

Accept the destination folder shown, or click the Browse button to choose a different folder for your installation, and then click the Next> button.

On the prompt for port numbers, accept the defaults, and then click the Next> button.

On the Passwords window, enter a password of your choice and confirm it, and then click the Next> button. The SYS and SYSTEM accounts created during this installation are for the database operation and administration, respectively. Note the password; you will use the SYSTEM account and its password for creating your own account, which you use for trying the examples.

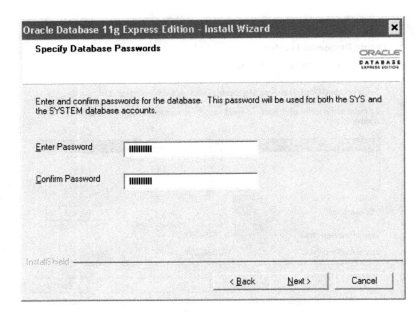

The Summary window will be displayed. Click Install.

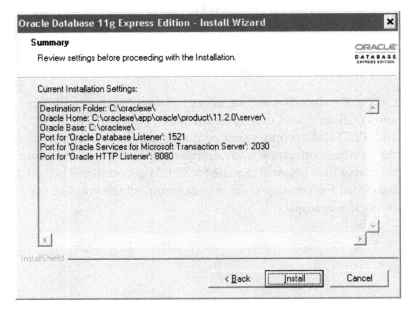

Finally, when the Installation Completion window appears, click the Finish button.

Your Oracle Database XE is now installed.

SQL Developer

SQL Developer is optional to try the book examples. Instead of using SQL Developer, you can run DDL on SQL*Plus for example. But I recommend using the GUI of the SQL Developer.

Go to http://www.oracle.com/technetwork/indexes/downloads/index.html

Locate and download the SQL Developer. You will be requested to accept the license agreement. If you don't have one, create an account; it's free.

Unzip the downloaded file to a folder of your preference. Note the folder name and its location; you will need to know them to start your SQL Developer.

When the unzipping is completed, look for the sqldeveloper.exe file.

You start SQL Developer by opening (double-clicking) this file.

You might want to create a short-cut on your Desktop.

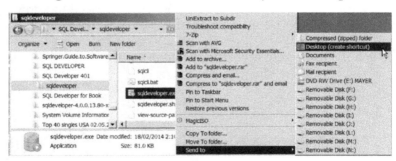

You can then start your SQL Developer by double-clicking the short-cut.

Your initial screen should look like the following. If you don't want to see the Start Page tab the next time you start SQL Developer, un-check the *Show on Startup* box at the bottom left side of the screen.

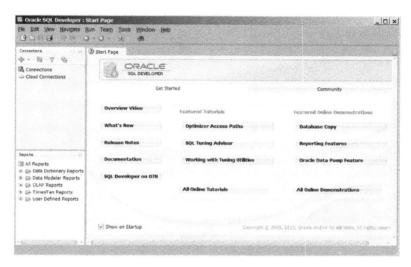

For now, close the Start Page tab by clicking its x.

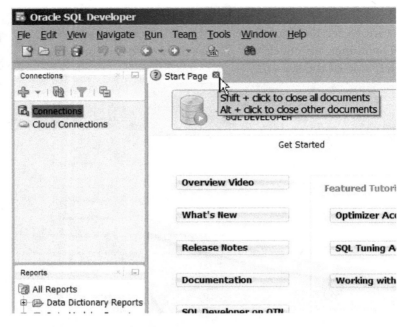

Creating Connection

To work with a database from SQL Developer, you need to have a connection.

A connection is specific to an account. As we will use the SYSTEM account to create your own account, you first have to create a connection for the SYSTEM account.

To create a connection, right-click the Connection folder.

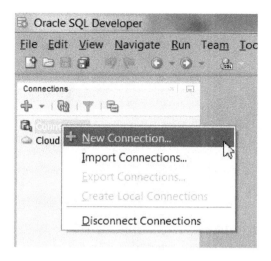

On the New/Select Database Connection window, enter a Connection Name and Username as shown. The Password is the password of SYSTEM account you entered during the Oracle database installation. Check the Save Password box.

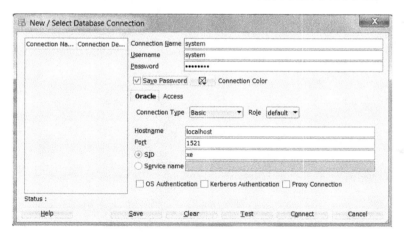

When you click the Connect button, the *system* connection you have just created should be available on the Connection Navigator.

A Worksheet is opened for the system connection. The Worksheet is where you type in source codes.

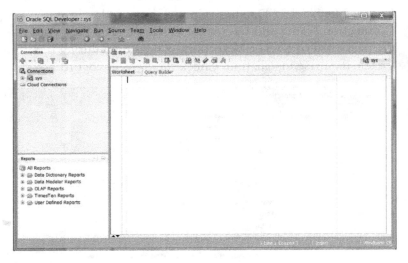

Appendix B: Preparing for the Book Examples

This appendix helps your preparation to try the book examples. It guides you to:
- Create users (accounts)
- Set up a connection
- Create and populate example tables.

Creating Accounts (Users)

We need two database accounts. The first account, *salesmanager,* will be the owner (creator) of the example tables. These tables are said to be in the salesmanager schema. We will use the other account, *ruser,* to explore metadata and write queries.

These two accounts kind of simulate what you encounter in real-world environment: the schema owner and the account given to you as an R user.

In your real-world environment your database administrator is responsible to create accounts. The R user is necessary as giving you the schema owner would be way too risky. The schema owner is too powerful an account, e.g. can wiped out tables.

Creating *salesmanager* account

To create a new account, expand the *system* connection and locate the Other Users folder at the bottom of the folder tree.

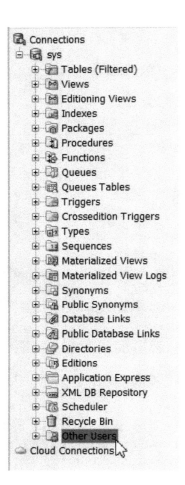

Right click and select Create User.

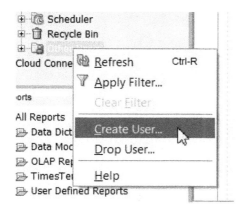

Enter a User Name of your choice, a password and its confirmation, and then click the Apply button. You should get a successful pop-up window; close it.

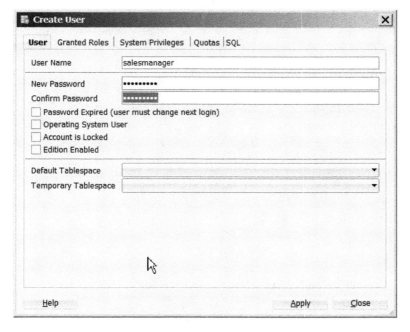

On the Granted Roles tab, click Grant All, Admin All and Default All buttons; then click the Apply button. Close the successful window and the Edit User as well.

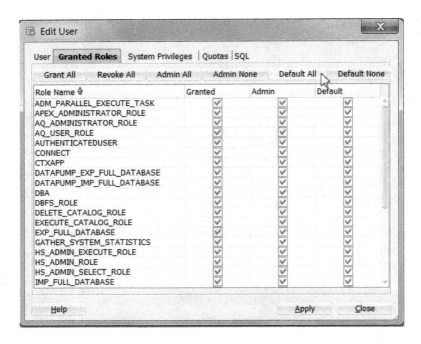

Creating *ruser* user

You create *ruser* the same as you did the salesmanager. The only differences are:

- Do not grant anything on the Grant Roles tab.
- But, on the System Privileges tab check the Granted box as shown below.

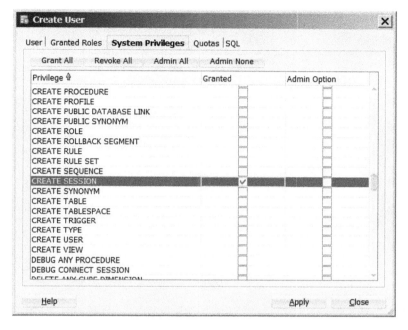

Create and populate the example tables

Here is the script (listing of SQL statements) to create and populate the example tables.

You can copy and paste the lines to SQL Developer worksheet and run them. If you buy print paper version of the book, you can email me requesting the script. My email is djoni.darmawikarta@gmail.com.

Connect as salesmanager and open a worksheet. When you have pasted the codes on the worksheet, run the script by clicking F5.

```
-- Create tables --
CREATE TABLE salesmanager.customer
   (
    c_no     NUMBER (2) NOT NULL ,
    c_name   VARCHAR2 (20 BYTE) NOT NULL ,
    address  VARCHAR2 (50 BYTE) ,
    city     VARCHAR2 (20 BYTE) ,
    prov     VARCHAR2 (20 BYTE) ,
    phone    VARCHAR2 (20 BYTE)
   )
    ;
CREATE UNIQUE INDEX salesmanager.customer_pk ON
salesmanager.customer
   (
    c_no ASC
   )
    ;
  GRANT
  SELECT ON salesmanager.customer TO ruser ;
ALTER TABLE salesmanager.customer ADD CONSTRAINT
customer_pk PRIMARY KEY ( c_no ) USING INDEX
salesmanager.customer_pk ;


CREATE TABLE salesmanager.c_order
   (
    c_no     NUMBER (2) NOT NULL ,
    p_code   VARCHAR2 (6 BYTE) NOT NULL ,
    qty      NUMBER (4) NOT NULL ,
    order_dt DATE NOT NULL ,
    SOURCE   VARCHAR2 (20 BYTE) ,
```

```
    subs      VARCHAR2 (6 BYTE)
  )
  ;
COMMENT ON COLUMN salesmanager.c_order.c_no
IS
  'A unique number assigned to every customer' ;
  COMMENT ON COLUMN salesmanager.c_order.p_code
IS
  'A unique code assigned to every product' ;
  COMMENT ON COLUMN salesmanager.c_order.qty
IS
  'Quantity of product ordered' ;
  COMMENT ON COLUMN salesmanager.c_order.order_dt
IS
  'The date the order we accepted' ;
  COMMENT ON COLUMN salesmanager.c_order.SOURCE
IS
  'The warehouse we supply the order from' ;
  COMMENT ON COLUMN salesmanager.c_order.subs
IS
  'A substitue product that can replace the product
ordered' ;
CREATE UNIQUE INDEX salesmanager.c_order_uk1 ON
salesmanager.c_order
  (
    c_no ASC , p_code ASC , order_dt ASC
  )
  ;
  GRANT
  SELECT ON salesmanager.c_order TO ruser ;
ALTER TABLE salesmanager.c_order ADD CONSTRAINT c_order_uk1
UNIQUE ( c_no , p_code , order_dt ) USING INDEX
salesmanager.c_order_uk1 ;


CREATE TABLE salesmanager.inv
  (
    warehouse VARCHAR2 (20 BYTE) NOT NULL ,
    p_code    VARCHAR2 (6 BYTE) ,
    qty       NUMBER (4)
  )
  ;
GRANT
SELECT ON salesmanager.inv TO ruser ;


CREATE TABLE salesmanager.product
  (
    p_code    VARCHAR2 (6 BYTE) NOT NULL ,
    p_name    VARCHAR2 (15 BYTE) NOT NULL ,
    price     NUMBER (4,2) ,
    launch_dt DATE ,
    subs      VARCHAR2 (6 BYTE)
  )
  ;
```

```
CREATE UNIQUE INDEX salesmanager.product_pk ON
salesmanager.product
  (
    p_code ASC
  )
  ;
  GRANT
  SELECT ON salesmanager.product TO ruser ;
ALTER TABLE salesmanager.product ADD CONSTRAINT product_pk
PRIMARY KEY ( p_code ) USING INDEX salesmanager.product_pk
;

CREATE TABLE salesmanager.shp
  (
    c_no     NUMBER (2) NOT NULL ,
    p_code   VARCHAR2 (6 BYTE) NOT NULL ,
    order_dt DATE NOT NULL ,
    qty      NUMBER (4) NOT NULL ,
    s_dt     DATE NOT NULL
  )
  ;
GRANT
SELECT ON salesmanager.shp TO ruser ;

ALTER TABLE salesmanager.c_order ADD CONSTRAINT c_order_fk1
FOREIGN KEY ( p_code ) REFERENCES salesmanager.product (
p_code ) NOT DEFERRABLE ;

ALTER TABLE salesmanager.c_order ADD CONSTRAINT c_order_fk2
FOREIGN KEY ( c_no ) REFERENCES salesmanager.customer (
c_no ) NOT DEFERRABLE ;

ALTER TABLE salesmanager.c_order ADD CONSTRAINT c_order_fk3
FOREIGN KEY ( subs ) REFERENCES salesmanager.product (
p_code ) NOT DEFERRABLE ;

ALTER TABLE salesmanager.shp ADD CONSTRAINT shp_fk1 FOREIGN
KEY ( c_no, p_code, order_dt ) REFERENCES
salesmanager.c_order ( c_no, p_code, order_dt ) NOT
DEFERRABLE ;

CREATE OR REPLACE PUBLIC SYNONYM customer FOR
salesmanager.customer ;

CREATE OR REPLACE PUBLIC SYNONYM c_order FOR
salesmanager.c_order ;

CREATE OR REPLACE SYNONYM inv FOR salesmanager.inv ;

CREATE OR REPLACE PUBLIC SYNONYM product FOR
salesmanager.product ;

CREATE OR REPLACE PUBLIC SYNONYM shp FOR salesmanager.shp ;

-- Populate tables --
```

```
-- customer
SET define OFF;
INSERT INTO salesmanager.customer
(c_no,c_name,address,city,prov) VALUES (10,'Standard
Store','10 University Ave','Toronto','ON');
INSERT INTO salesmanager.customer
(c_no,c_name,address,city,prov) VALUES (20,'Quality
Store','20 Windham Street','Toronto','ON');
INSERT INTO salesmanager.customer
(c_no,c_name,address,city,prov) VALUES (30,'Head
Office','30 Burbank Dr','North York','ON');
INSERT INTO salesmanager.customer
(c_no,c_name,address,city,prov) VALUES (40,'Super
Agent','40 Palomino Ave','North York','ON');
-- product
INSERT INTO salesmanager.product
(p_code,p_name,price,launch_dt,subs) VALUES
('1','Nail',10,to_date('15-03-31','RR-MM-DD'),NULL);
INSERT INTO salesmanager.product
(p_code,p_name,price,launch_dt,subs) VALUES
('2','Washer',15,to_date('13-03-29','RR-MM-DD'),NULL);
INSERT INTO salesmanager.product
(p_code,p_name,price,launch_dt,subs) VALUES
('3','Nut',15,to_date('13-03-29','RR-MM-DD'),NULL);
INSERT INTO salesmanager.product
(p_code,p_name,price,launch_dt,subs) VALUES
('4','Screw',25,to_date('13-03-30','RR-MM-DD'),'5');
INSERT INTO salesmanager.product
(p_code,p_name,price,launch_dt,subs) VALUES
('5','Super_Nut',30,to_date('13-03-30','RR-MM-DD'),NULL);
INSERT INTO salesmanager.product
(p_code,p_name,price,launch_dt,subs) VALUES ('6','New
Nut',NULL,NULL,NULL);
-- inv
INSERT INTO salesmanager.inv (warehouse,p_code,qty) VALUES
('1','1',100);
INSERT INTO salesmanager.inv (warehouse,p_code,qty) VALUES
('2','2',200);
-- c_order
SET define OFF;
INSERT INTO salesmanager.c_order
(c_no,p_code,qty,order_dt,SOURCE,subs) VALUES
(10,'1',100,to_date('13-04-01','RR-MM-DD'),'1',NULL);
INSERT INTO salesmanager.c_order
(c_no,p_code,qty,order_dt,SOURCE,subs) VALUES
(10,'2',100,to_date('13-04-01','RR-MM-DD'),'1','1');
INSERT INTO salesmanager.c_order
(c_no,p_code,qty,order_dt,SOURCE,subs) VALUES
(20,'1',200,to_date('13-04-01','RR-MM-DD'),'2',NULL);
INSERT INTO salesmanager.c_order
(c_no,p_code,qty,order_dt,SOURCE,subs) VALUES
(30,'3',300,to_date('13-04-02','RR-MM-DD'),'2',NULL);
```

```
INSERT INTO salesmanager.c_order
(c_no,p_code,qty,order_dt,SOURCE,subs) VALUES
(40,'4',400,to_date('13-04-02','RR-MM-DD'),NULL,NULL);
INSERT INTO salesmanager.c_order
(c_no,p_code,qty,order_dt,SOURCE,subs) VALUES
(40,'5',400,to_date('13-04-03','RR-MM-DD'),NULL,'4');
-- shp
INSERT INTO salesmanager.shp
(c_no,p_code,order_dt,qty,s_dt) VALUES (10,'1',to_date('13-
04-01','RR-MM-DD'),100,to_date('13-04-05','RR-MM-DD'));
INSERT INTO salesmanager.shp
(c_no,p_code,order_dt,qty,s_dt) VALUES (10,'2',to_date('13-
04-01','RR-MM-DD'),100,to_date('13-04-05','RR-MM-DD'));
-- end of script --
```

Appendix C: Indexing

Book index helps you find the page that contains a word faster. Similarly, a column index of a table can speed up your finding data in a database. If your query has a condition on a column that is not indexed, the table will be fully scanned and the query will be slower than if an index on that column is available.

Once you have the queries, you might need to talk the system/application/database administrator to get their help creating indexes. You will need to show and explain the queries.

An index does not need to be on just a column. Consider the following case. A query has to search on the p_name column of the product table and there can be more than one row with the same p_name but with different launch dates. In this case, the query can be faster if a multi-column index on both p_name and launch_dt is available.

Function based index is another type of index, which is especially useful if your query uses a function in the WHERE condition. In the following query, for example, we use the UPPER function.

```
SELECT * FROM customer WHERE UPPER(c_name) LIKE
    '%STORE';
```

An index on UPPER(c_name) instead of just the c_name column will have greater impact on the speed of the query.

Appendix D: Built-in Functions

The Oracle database provides functions that you can use in your queries. These built-in functions can be grouped into numeric functions, character functions, datetime functions, and functions for handling null values. The objective of this chapter is to introduce you to some of these functions.

Numeric Functions

The following are some of the more important numeric functions.

ABS

ABS(n) returns the absolute value of n. For example, the following query returns the absolute value of (price - 20.00) as the third column.

```
Worksheet    Query Builder
1    SELECT p_code, price, (price - 20), ABS(price - 20.00) FROM product;
```

```
Query Result ×
SQL    All Rows Fetched: 6 in 0.031 seconds
```

	P_CODE	PRICE	(PRICE-20)	ABS(PRICE-20.00)
1	1	10	-10	10
2	2	15	-5	5
3	3	15	-5	5
4	4	25	5	5
5	5	30	10	10
6	6	(null)	(null)	(null)

ROUND

ROUND(n, d) returns a number rounded to a certain number of decimal places. The argument n is the number to be rounded and *d* the number of decimal places. For example, the following query uses ROUND to round price to one decimal place.

Worksheet	Query Builder
1	SELECT p_code, price * 0.33, ROUND (price * 0.33, 1) FROM product;

Query Result ×

SQL   All Rows Fetched: 6 in 0.015 seconds

P_CODE	PRICE*0.33	ROUND(PRICE*0.33,1)
1 1	3.3	3.3
2 2	4.95	5
3 3	4.95	5
4 4	8.25	8.3
5 5	9.9	9.9
6 6	(null)	(null)

SIGN

SIGN(n) returns a value indicating the sign of n. This function returns -1 for $n < 0$, 0 for $n = 0$, and 1 for $n > 0$. As an example, the following query uses SIGN to return the sign of (price – 15).

Worksheet	Query Builder
1	SELECT p_code, price, SIGN(price - 15) FROM product;

Query Result ×

SQL   All Rows Fetched: 6 in 0.031 seconds

P_CODE	PRICE	SIGN(PRICE-15)
1 1	10	-1
2 2	15	0
3 3	15	0
4 4	25	1
5 5	30	1
6 6	(null)	(null)

TRUNC

TRUNC(n, d) returns a number truncated to a certain number of decimal places. The argument n is the number to truncate and d the number of decimal places. For example, the following query truncates price to one decimal place.

```
Worksheet    Query Builder
  1   SELECT p_code, price * 0.33, TRUNC(price * 0.33, 1) FROM product;
```

Query Result ×

SQL | All Rows Fetched: 6 in 0 seconds

P_CODE	PRICE*0.33	TRUNC(PRICE*0.33,1)
1 1	3.3	3.3
2 2	4.95	4.9
3 3	4.95	4.9
4 4	8.25	8.2
5 5	9.9	9.9
6 6	(null)	(null)

Character Functions

The following are some of the more important string functions.

CONCAT

CONCAT(*string1*, *string2*) concatenates *string1* and *string2* and returns the result. If you pass a number as an argument, the number will first be converted to a string. In the following example three strings, *p_name*, a dash, and *description*, are concatenated.

Note that the price column value will be converted automatically to a string.

```
Worksheet    Query Builder
  1  SELECT p_code, CONCAT(CONCAT(p_name, ' -- ') , price) FROM product;
```

▲▼
▷ Query Result ×

📌 🖨 📑 📑 SQL | All Rows Fetched: 6 in 0 seconds

P_CODE	CONCAT(CONCAT(P_NAME,'--'),PRICE)
1 1	Nail -- 10
2 2	Washer -- 15
3 3	Nut -- 15
4 4	Screw -- 25
5 5	Super_Nut -- 30
6 6	New Nut --

You can also use the || operator to concatenate strings. The following query produces the same output as the one above.

```
SELECT p_code, p_name || ' -- ' || price FROM
     product;
```

LOWER and UPPER

LOWER(*str*) converts *str* to lowercase and UPPER(*str*) converts *str* to uppercase. For example, the following query uses LOWER and UPPER.

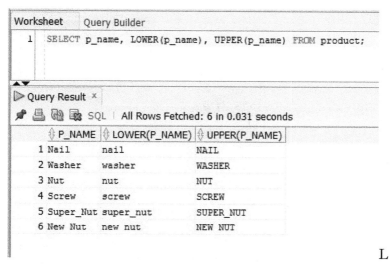

L

LENGTH

LENGTH(*str*) returns the length of string *str*. The length of a string is the number of characters in it. For example, the following query returns the length of p_name as the second column.

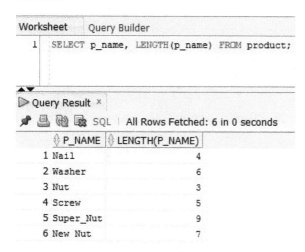

SUBSTR

SUBSTR(*str*, *start_position*, [*length*]) returns a substring of *str* starting from the position indicated by *start_position*. If *length* is not specified, the function returns a substring from *start_position* to the last character in *str*. If *length* is present, the function returns a substring which is *length* characters long starting from *start_position*. If *length* is less than 1, the function returns an empty string.

Assuming the customer tables has the rows with the phone numbers as shown. The query will return the substrings of the phone numbers starting from position 7 to the end.

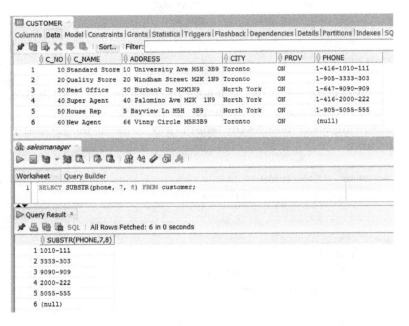

Datetime Functions

The following are some of the more important datetime functions.

CURRENT_DATE

CURRENT_DATE() returns the current date (the current date of the Oracle server at the time you run the query). For instance, the following query will return a result that looks like this.

The actual value of the third column will depend on when you run the query, which in my case is 18 January 2016.

Worksheet	Query Builder
1	SELECT p_code, launch_dt, CURRENT_DATE FROM product;

▲▼

▷ Query Result ˣ

🔹 🖨 🔁 🗟 SQL ⏐ All Rows Fetched: 6 in 0 seconds

	⇕ P_CODE	⇕ LAUNCH_DT	⇕ CURRENT_DATE
1	1	15-03-31	16-01-18
2	2	13-03-29	16-01-18
3	3	13-03-29	16-01-18
4	4	13-03-30	16-01-18
5	5	13-03-30	16-01-18
6	6	(null)	16-01-18

TO_CHAR

TO_CHAR(*dt*, *fmt_specifier*) converts a date (*dt*) to a string in the format specified by *fmt_specifier*. In the following example, the launch_dt column is formatted with a format specifier that has three components:

- DD - the day of the month
- MONTH - the long name of the month in uppercase
- YYYY - the year

```
Worksheet    Query Builder
  1   SELECT p_code,
  2      TO_CHAR(launch_dt, 'DD MONTH YYYY') reformatted_dt
  3   FROM product;
  4
```

▲▼
▷ Query Result ✕

📌 🖨 🔃 ⬛ SQL | All Rows Fetched: 6 in 0 seconds

	◊ P_CODE	◊ REFORMATTED_DT
1	1	31 MARCH 2015
2	2	29 MARCH 2013
3	3	29 MARCH 2013
4	4	30 MARCH 2013
5	5	30 MARCH 2013
6	6	(null)

NULL-related functions

The following are some of the functions that can be used to handle null values.

COALESCE

COALESCE(*expr-1*, *expr-2*, ..., *expr-n*) returns the first expression from the list that is not NULL.

For example, suppose your product table contains the following three prices. The query with the COALESCE function will pick any one price in the parameters that is first available (not null) in the sequence listed.

	P_CODE	P_NAME	PRICE	LAUNCH_DT	SUBS	SUBS_PRICE	MARKET_PRICE
1	1	Nail	10	15-03-31	(null)	(null)	11
2	2	Washer	15	13-03-29	(null)	(null)	15
3	3	Nut	15	13-03-29	(null)	(null)	16
4	4	Screw	(null)	13-03-30	(null)	(null)	22
5	5	Super_Nut	(null)	13-03-30	6	30	10
6	6	New Nut	30	(null)	5	(null)	30

salesmanager

Worksheet   Query Builder

```
1  SELECT p_name, COALESCE(price , subs_price, market_price) FROM product;
2
```

Query Result ×

SQL   All Rows Fetched: 6 in 0 seconds

	P_NAME	COALESCE(PRICE,SUBS_PRICE,MARKET_PRICE)
1	Nail	10
2	Washer	15
3	Nut	15
4	Screw	22
5	Super_Nut	30
6	New Nut	30

NULLIF

NULLIF (*expr1*, *expr2*) compares *expr1* and *expr2*. If they are equal, the function returns null. If they are not equal, the function returns *expr1*.

Here is an example. Note that comparing anything to null results to null, i.e. the case with row number 4 and 5 on the Query Output. See the next function, NVL.

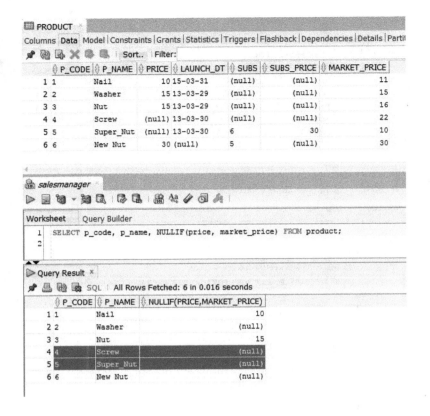

NVL

NVL (*expr1*, *expr2*) returns *exprs1* if *expr1* is not NULL; otherwise, it returns *expr2*.

The following query employs the NVL function to pick any one of the market prices if the price is null.

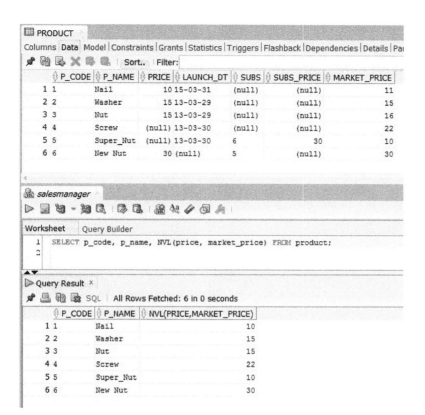

Index